Speaking the Piano

Speaking the Piano

Reflections on
Learning and Teaching

Susan Tomes

THE BOYDELL PRESS

First published 2018
The Boydell Press, Woodbridge

ISBN 978 1 78327 325 6

The Boydell Press is an imprint of Boydell & Brewer Ltd
PO Box 9, Woodbridge, Suffolk IP12 3DF, UK
and of Boydell & Brewer Inc.
668 Mt Hope Avenue, Rochester, NY 14620–2731, USA
website: www.boydellandbrewer.com

A CIP catalogue record for this book is available
from the British Library

The publisher has no responsibility for the continued existence or
accuracy of URLs for external or third-party internet websites referred to
in this book, and does not guarantee that any content on such websites is,
or will remain, accurate or appropriate

This publication is printed on acid-free paper

Contents

'You must speak the piano'
Theodor Leschetizky to Artur Schnabel,
as reported by Clifford Curzon

Acknowledgements

I am very grateful to my husband Robert Philip and to my friend Deborah Valenze for reading the manuscript of this book at various stages and giving me wise advice as well as encouragement. Michael Middeke at Boydell Press gave valuable editorial guidance. I am grateful also to the members of my Piano Club, who have stimulated useful thoughts about how much one can learn from playing the piano. Most of the great teachers I've written about – György Sebök, Sándor Végh, Jaki Byard – are, sadly, no longer with us. But the performers of Alba Flamenca are as large as life if not larger. May they go from strength to strength!

Introduction

Playing music is a craft, but unlike many other crafts there's nothing tangible to show for it when you've finished – no clay pot you've made on the wheel, no table to put your coffee cup on, no sweater to wear in winter, no flower border in the garden. Any child who gets up early to practise a musical instrument before school, any adult amateur who carves out precious time from their day job in order to play the piano, will probably have been struck by the realisation that – contrary to the hobbies enjoyed by their friends – the time they spend on practising just seems to vanish without trace. For unlike other crafts whose aim is to produce a beautiful or useful object, the craft of music-making is concerned with *evoking* something. To do so, it uses elements of athleticism, mathematics and pattern recognition, but the goal is beyond that.

There is enormous pleasure in developing the physical skill needed to play or sing; the process is satisfying enough in itself to claim many musicians' attention for years. Some teachers make their reputation by specialising in technique, and libraries are full of books about the physical aspects of playing instruments. But as listeners, we all know that when music strikes us or moves us it is not because someone has played accurately or with correct posture and use of weight. It's because through the medium of sound we have been put in touch with feelings, beauty, and the world of the spirit. Yes, a musician needs physical skill to access these realms, but physical skill is not enough; musicians have to be sensitive to how the notes and sounds can act as portals into other dimensions. Luckily, a musician with even the simplest technique can start reaching into those dimensions.

How do we teach such things? Although there are 'methods' for learning to play instruments, learning to awaken the imagination is a subtle process, one which, as Donald Tovey pointed out in his commentary on Beethoven's piano sonatas, is work for the whole person. Despite the lack of straightforward recipes, teaching should always address the question of what we are trying to achieve beyond good tuning, tone and stage presence. Such matters are difficult to put into words, but there are many ways of alerting a student to what lies beyond the notes on the page. Sometimes, just listening to someone else play can give you a clue as to how to take the next step. At other times, a teacher's well-chosen words can spark off your imagination. As a student myself I was often struck by the apt metaphors and images used by the best of my teachers, whose skill with words inspired me to search for ways to express what is going on when we engage with music. Not everyone wishes to apply words to music, but some people find that words turn the key and open the door. I'm fortunate that my life as a performer has given me a treasury of experiences on which to draw when discussing music and how to make it speak.

Learning to make music means learning to hear the sound you are making. This may seem obvious, but in fact many pianists (for example) find it very difficult to sit back and hear their sound as it actually is, and as listeners hear it. In this respect, music is different from an art like dance, because although dancers know what they are doing and experience the joy of movement through space, they cannot *see* the result on stage as the audience can. In music we *can* immediately hear the result of our efforts, but sometimes we are so immersed in the physical process that we forget to listen. When I started teaching I was amazed at what a large proportion of the time was taken up with making people aware of the sound they were actually making. They seemed to identify so strongly with the sensation of playing or pattern-making that they simply left the sound to take care of itself. The piano, one of the largest of musical instruments, often seems an intimidating partner in the music-making enterprise. Many pianists seem to believe that it, not they, is responsible for the sound. But although the sound comes from the piano, the character of the sound is determined by the pianist. We pianists have to realise that we are the ones in charge. *As we play, so shall the sound be.* When people are led to this realisation, it can have a profound impact on their playing.

For years after I turned professional as a performer, I continued to learn in masterclasses and seminars. I encountered some very important teachers and through them, some inspiring musical goals. When I started to receive invitations to teach others, I found that teaching was surprisingly like continuing to be a learner, only in another guise. As a teacher, I felt I was seeing the learning process from another point on the spectrum, but it didn't suddenly become a different spectrum. What was being taught, what was being learned: these were bound up with one another in some kind of creative circle. Yes, I had more experience than my students, and had grappled more with the issues, but I also learned some things from them, and we shared our conclusions about how to cope with life in music. I have sometimes observed that when people become teachers, they seem almost deliberately to 'put away childish things' and to lose contact with what it was like to be a student. I didn't feel that way. The violinist Sándor Végh used to say that we were all 'links in a chain' of centuries-old musical understanding, and I felt the truth of that when I came to share my thoughts with others. Teaching and learning for me have been a continuum.

When I started giving my own masterclasses, I invited members of the public to come and listen. If they were new to such classes, they were surprised by what we were talking about. They had imagined (they said) that they might have to sit through endless discussion of technical matters, and perhaps some advice on how to present oneself on the platform. Naturally there was some of that, but most of the time we were discussing musical shape and meaning, what atmosphere the composer was trying to create, how the energy of the music flowed, and how to vary the tone and touch so that our playing matched what was going on in the music. In fact, we were most likely to be discussing something like what *sort* of loud or soft was needed here, and why. I think some of our listeners had supposed that there was a Right Way to play a piece of classical music, and that we all aspired to be able to play it in that way. The more accomplished we were, the closer we'd be able to get to perfection. In the classes they were struck by the realisation that there wasn't a one-size-fits-all solution: every note involved making choices and confronting your own skills. Each musician would refract the music through their own understanding and their own physique, using their own palette of colours and bringing out aspects of the music which seemed important to them. How we played it would profoundly affect how listeners heard it. Once they had realised that, they started to join us in imagination as we entered the labyrinth of decisions that led us deeper into the heart of the music.

Section One

Teaching

Enlisting the imagination

A couple of years ago I started a monthly Piano Club for adult amateur pianists who play for fun, but are serious about their playing and want to develop their skills. Being a pianist can be quite a lonely thing because piano music tends to be self-sufficient; playing melody and harmony at the same time, you don't need other people to play with you to complete the musical picture. Chamber music has given me a welcome opportunity to socialise with other musicians, but not with other pianists. I've always rather regretted this, because pianists are a special type of musician and might be good friends if they could get over the feeling that they must each defend their hard-won territory. But professional pianists don't have much occasion to socialise with one another, and I realised that I had very little interaction with amateur pianists either. Knowing how many people there are who take their piano playing to quite a high level before diverting into other professions, I felt there must surely be plenty of potential 'takers' for a forum in which we could meet to exchange ideas and experiences. In adult life many amateurs stop having piano lessons, but that doesn't mean they have stopped being interested in music or wanting to play better. I put out the word and within a few weeks I had collected enough participants to begin.

Amateur and professional pianists often seem like very different animals. One might think that the only difference between us is that some of us get paid for playing music, but in fact there are many other differences. There's something about the intensity of involvement and the level of responsibility you feel as a professional, plus the degree of scrutiny you attract, which gradually changes your whole relationship to music (and perhaps also changes you yourself) in a rather complicated way. I often regret that non-professionals don't have more insight into the concerns of professional performers. Playing a piano piece because you like it is very different from working on it with minute attention to detail because you want to reach a global standard of excellence and be recognised and remembered for your particular way of doing things. It brings you into a daily struggle with perfectionism which, despite its benefits, can make you feel rather separate from those around you. So when I started Piano Club I admit I was partly motivated by the thought that I could explain myself to a few more people who would then have a deeper appreciation of what they were hearing and what was going on in the performer's mind when they came to concerts. Fortunately, as it turned out, some of the people interested in attending Piano Club had a matching wish to find out what made a pianist like me 'tick'.

For each meeting the members of Piano Club prepare pieces to play to me in front of one another, to get some feedback and advice (and to have coffee and home-made cake). It's been a fascinating experience for me, because I'm constantly learning about the many different ways in which music-making can be important to people. To some, the music itself is the most important thing. To others, making music is the attraction, often because it involves social interaction. Some are fascinated by the physical task of playing the piano, and don't care whether anyone hears them or not. Some hope that the piano will give them the opportunity for a public platform, while others treat it as a refuge from engaging with other people. Some people hope the piano will talk for them. I've seen how much effort it costs some people to play in public, even if the public is a small group of like-minded individuals. I've also seen the different relationships that pianists have to the piano itself with its enormous imposing bulk and its air of heroic solitude. People's posture and body language often change when they sit down at a grand piano, and before they have played a note one can tell something about them from watching how boldly or timidly – or indeed how happily – they take their place in front of the instrument. It's always fascinating to hear people play for the first time. Although you may have gained an impression of their personality from speaking to them or corresponding with them, you frequently hear a different side of them – an important side – when they play. It often feels as if there must be a different circuit between brain and hand than there is between brain and words.

In their working lives, many of my Piano Club members are high-powered individuals with specialist skills. I enjoy working with them because they are quick to absorb new concepts or to grasp underlying principles, and they often make rapid progress. They're all passionate about music and have maintained impressive playing ability despite having very limited time to practise. Some of them, in fact, came close to choosing music as a career and still fantasise about what might have been. They all say that their piano playing has been of benefit to them not only in their working lives but also in the context of their health and well-being. I admire them for taking the time to prepare pieces to play at Piano Club and am well aware that I have no way of reciprocating their commitment by joining (for example) their Saturday Amateur Surgery Club.

I often envy them because they decided to keep music as a hobby. I adore music, but for me, playing the piano is no longer the simple pleasure it was when I was a child. I'd like to say I play the piano every day because I want to, but in fact I also do it because it is my livelihood, and it's my duty to keep my playing in good order. As Liszt (or, according to some people, the Polish pianist Ignacy Jan Paderewski) is reported to have said, 'If I miss one day of practice, I notice it; if I miss two days, the critics notice it, and if I miss three days, the public notices it.' We worry that our fine control may not remain absolutely at our command. It may be an exaggerated sensitivity, but it feels real.

Some of my Piano Club members do have performance opportunities, but they have never had to associate music with earning a living. They don't have to worry about what fee they can or cannot command, how their playing compares to global standards, or whether they might have to endure the thought of the nation reading about their shortcomings in the newspapers. As a professional musician I'm rarely free from such concerns. Even when I sight-read pieces for fun, I can't help inwardly calculating what it would take to bring them up to performance standard. This is not a concern for members of Piano Club, because most people who come to hear them play know them as mums and dads, doctors, teachers, grannies and grandpas, and don't expect them to be perfect. They play out of sheer love of music and it rubs off on me. I like it that when they sit down to play, they often begin by saying how much they love the piece they're working on.

It has made me realise that in the professional world of classical music, there is tremendous emphasis on the *end result*. The goal is to be ready for the concert when it comes, and frankly the concert is the only thing that counts. All the work leading up to it is hidden away and filed under the heading of 'getting ready'. Musicians practise and practise, but their practice is the equivalent of all the messy threads that you see if you look behind a beautiful tapestry: essential to the end product, but not meant to be seen. In other fields, such as the visual arts, the public takes enormous interest in artists' states of mind and in the trials and errors that become ingredients in their artworks, but musicians are rarely asked about the time we spend learning our craft, polishing our physical skills, interpreting and memorising the music. Perhaps we have too successfully sold, even to ourselves, the notion that classical musicians appear magically on the concert platform in a glow of perfection. No one wants to hear about the sleepless hours we spend going over the repertoire in our heads, practising the fingering on café tables, worrying about our nerves. Our self-imposed task is to make the finished result look as effortless as possible, and the long process of preparation is a means to an end, not an end in itself. For my Piano Club people, on the other hand, the process *is* an end in itself. They are not obsessed with reaching a polished result, partly because there is no particular place in their busy lives for a piece of piano music burnished to a high gloss. They enjoy experiencing the stages that a pianist has to go through when learning a piece they love, and are happy to compare notes with one another on those experiences.

When Piano Club first started, and before I had heard any of the prospective members, I asked people to send me lists of the pieces they wanted to play. I concluded from their responses that they must all be advanced pianists. In fact, it wasn't as simple as that. Some of them turned out to be advanced, and others less so, but it made no difference to the level of difficulty they wanted to tackle. I realised that their musical understanding was more highly developed than their playing technique. Bringing this music into their lives was the important thing. They wanted to spend time with it, hear some other ideas about it and get a glimpse of how a professional pianist would approach it. They didn't see why they should be barred from attempting it just because it was 'too difficult for them' or because they didn't have time to practise it. I was used to teaching full-time students and young professionals who wouldn't dare to bring a difficult piece to a lesson unless they could 'play it properly'. It was a new experience to have people stumble through the classics in front of me, but I quickly saw that *engaging with music* was the important thing. At coffee break I'd realise from the heightened colour in their cheeks that it had cost them considerable effort to play in front of the others.

During these coffee breaks it's often observed that 'everything was fine at home, but seems to go wrong when the rest of you are listening'. We all agree that when piano playing changes from a private to a public activity, unpredictable things happen. Knowing things 'well enough' is not the same as being secure enough for public performance. Of course most people have experience of having to speak in public or make presentations for work, but usually such public appearances involve speaking, rather than performing something as intricate as a Chopin nocturne or a Schubert impromptu, where trembling hands are an operational problem. People often say that things they have never, ever had trouble with before suddenly develop thorns and trip them up. Things they thought they knew from memory can just vanish into the air like steam. A mean little voice in their head whispers to them, 'you can't do this'. They're startled by this voice, which seems to keep silent until the very moment they need to feel confident. They look to me for reassurance that such things don't happen to more seasoned performers, but I have to tell them that – for me, and I guess for most performers – fighting against those little voices is a constant challenge. In my view the best strategy is to be well prepared, and I find I have to point this out repeatedly, especially to those who pride themselves on being able to do things on their wits. No matter how quick you are or how daring, the performance arena bristles with unexpected challenges. Many people are surprised for example to discover that their breathing goes haywire when they play to other people. Others are taken aback to find that their mental mapping of the keyboard becomes shaky when others are watching them play. A high or low note that they usually find without problems can suddenly seem to be ludicrously far away.

I turned over various ideas about how to help them. In a 'hobby' forum like this it wasn't appropriate to plunge into technical issues as one might in an individual lesson, partly because everyone else was listening and the last thing I wanted to do was to deplete anyone's confidence. Sometimes it seemed to me that the most important thing to do was simply to affirm each person in whatever they had managed to achieve in the time available, but I also realised that constant praise would quickly lose its charm. After all, they were there because they wanted new information. Obviously they weren't in a position to do day-by-day technical practice. Even if they had had the time to do so, some of them were facing a range of issues – such as arthritis or dyslexia – which placed limits on their progress in a physical sense. Yet they were all highly intelligent people and there was no limit to their ability to *appreciate* the music. Somehow we had to find ways of bridging the gap between their pianistic skills and their musical understanding. I noticed that people often fell into the habit of playing something over and over again in the same way, as though their lack of time and the fact that they no longer had a teacher obliged them to stay at a certain level, repeating pieces they liked without really believing that they could ever play them better. As I listened I sometimes suspected that they had been playing these pieces in this way for a considerable period of time. I knew that they didn't have much time to devote to piano practice, but I felt sure they could benefit from a bit of what I recently heard a neuroscientist call 'mentalising'. Mentalising means trying to 'read' and understand the thoughts and feelings of other people even if those feelings are not immediately apparent. A piece of piano music is not another person, but I felt that the same exercise would be useful. Behind the inscrutable face of the black and white printed page, what feelings were latent? What would the music say to us if it could?

In a sense, I wanted my Piano Club members to cultivate a touch of impatience so that they weren't too comfortable dwelling for long periods of time in the 'over and over again' stage. Playing things over and over is an indispensable part of developing muscle memory, but mechanical practice needs to be accompanied by 'conceptual practice' where you evolve ideas about the form and character of the music. Even if they were only learning a piece for fun, and had no particular date by which they needed to have it ready, I wanted them to develop an appetite for the next stage of musical understanding. They wanted this too, but claimed that 'how to practise' was a subject that had been notably absent from their piano lessons in earlier years. One attribute they all possessed, and which was not impacted by age or physical problems, was imagination. But although they might possess imagination in a broad sense, I often found that they had never been encouraged to develop their ability to use their imagination when playing music.

All musicians can benefit from using their imagination, but for pianists there is a special reason to develop their imaginative powers because they have to play so many different pianos. Usually people have a piano to practise on at home, but that is the only place they get to play that particular instrument. If they play anywhere else, they have to play whatever instrument is there, and other pianos may feel and sound substantially different from the one they're used to. Members of Piano Club, for example, are always commenting on how 'thrown' they are by my Steinway C grand piano which 'puts them off their stroke'. The reality is that pianists (unlike many other instrumentalists) cannot allow themselves to depend on a particular instrument and its sound. I know string players who feel spiritually diminished if they are separated from their own beloved instrument, but this is not an attitude that pianists can afford to indulge in. Instead, they have to develop a strong enough image of what they're aiming at musically that it will endure no matter what piano they are called upon to play. They must learn to conjure up this image before they begin. It may seem surprising that people need to be reminded to start imagining music before they begin to play, but many of them do need reminding. I ascribe this to the fact that many people don't sufficiently realise that music is not independent of them. Time and again I see them starting to play 'from cold', as it were, without having a clear sense of the mood they want to create or the sound they want to hear. They seem just to start playing and wait to see what comes out, which may or may not be to their liking. If it is not to their liking, they feel discouraged. It's helpful to remind people that by 'mentalising' they can start the music flowing before they play a note. When they try to imagine the ideal sound, in the silence before they begin, you can see their physical attitude changing and the sound changing as a consequence. As they begin to play, they feel as if they are *joining in*. From the perspective of a listener, it's usually easy to spot the pianist who knows how to launch themselves on an imaginary current of music.

Pretending to be other people

When Piano Club gathered recently, I heard one of them telling the others about a marvellous piano recital he had attended at the Edinburgh International Festival. It was given by the dazzling young Russian pianist Daniil Trifonov. My student waxed lyrical about how Trifonov made light of the immense technical difficulties in his programme, appearing to devote himself entirely to the musical line and giving the impression that the tumbling virtuoso passages were as easy as falling off a log.

Later that morning at Piano Club it was this person's turn to play to me. He made rather heavy weather of certain passages, using the beats to mark time audibly. He didn't seem to be hearing the long beautiful phrases which were the chief delight of this music. It was easy to guess that mere repetition had been his default setting when practising. Rather disarmingly he explained to us that because he had been so busy at work, he 'had not had time to think about the music'. Practising the notes was challenge enough!

I was standing beside him in order to turn the pages. When he ground to a halt in the middle of a tricky passage, I quietly said to him, 'How would Trifonov play this?' He looked startled. 'How would Trifonov play it?' he mused. He lifted his head and gazed into the middle distance. Then he turned back to the keyboard. 'He would probably play it something like …', and he took a deep breath and whooshed lightly and elegantly through the very passage which had stumped him. Everyone in the room burst out laughing because the improvement was so dramatic. The pianist himself joined in the laughter.

This little scene provided plenty of food for thought. The obvious question was: if people are capable of playing better, why don't they do it in the first place? Even attempting to answer this question requires a profound understanding of psychology. When I told my Piano Club student to imitate someone he admired, I hadn't played a cheap trick on him. By enlisting his imagination I had given him permission to step outside of his usual habits for a moment. As he pondered my question he probably imagined himself actually *being* Daniil Trifonov and tried to channel that feeling of mastery. Because he was safely among friends, he didn't feel self-conscious about playing this game; for a few moments he was able to borrow that feeling of mastery and inhabit it. Moreover, he didn't have time to ask himself whether or not he could do it. He just did it.

I could probably have achieved more or less the same effect by suggesting that he modify elements of his posture, weight, touch, speed of attack on the piano keys, and so on. Instead of starting from square one, however, cautiously steering him through incremental steps of improvement which might have occupied us for many sessions to come, I jumped straight to the end result and suggested that he imagine himself achieving it there and then. Such a technique doesn't work with everyone, and has to be used sparingly, but when the moment is right it's a fantastic 'trick' to use because it causes a minor sensation amongst everyone listening. When you are pretending to be someone else, some of the things you do 'as them' may feel surprisingly natural, even if it hasn't occurred to you to do them like that before. If indeed these new things turn out to feel 'like you', you will have discovered something helpful about yourself, and you can incorporate those things into your own playing without feeling fraudulent. With luck the experience of 'being Trifonov' or whoever will leave some kind of permanent trace, a reminder that progress *can* sometimes be sudden and easy.

When I was a young professional I once had a couple of lessons with the wonderful Romanian pianist Radu Lupu. During the lessons, he demonstrated how he felt certain passages should go. It was delightful to be so near him while he played and I observed him closely. After one of those lessons, my flatmates asked me what he had told me. To amuse them, I sat down at the piano and imitated Radu's style of playing those passages, imitating (as best I could) his sense of timing, his way of driving through a passage, his dramatic shifts of dynamic, his way of leaning back against the back of the chair, even his stern expression. My friends were entranced – disturbingly entranced. 'Go on!' they implored. 'That's great!' I felt a bit chagrined. Was my imitation of Radu Lupu so much better than my own playing? If so, should I carry on playing 'like him'? I didn't know what to think. Obviously my piano playing did not magically improve at the moment I decided to imitate Radu. I still had my own sound, which my flatmates heard every day when I practised, and seemed to take in their stride. Why were they suddenly so impressed? It had to be to do with body language and projection of some kind of aura. I realised that perhaps when I tried to 'be Radu Lupu' I was copying the outward signs of absolute self-belief and confidence in my right to hold an audience's attention, and my friends were subconsciously responding to that.

Displaying the outward signs was not, however, the same as feeling them inwardly. At that stage of my development I was still trying to find my voice and build my confidence. When I was on the concert platform I probably looked as if I was pleading with the audience to like me. Radu Lupu didn't look like that at all: his aura was magisterial. It seemed that I could imitate it, at least for the purposes of a demonstration. But I knew that to continue imitating Radu Lupu would be sterile, doomed to be nothing more than a tribute act. Perhaps I could try to incorporate his body language into my own platform manner? But I felt that would be a purely cosmetic change and easily identifiable as such. Instead, I tried to divine what the underlying principles of Radu's playing were. That was a better decision which made it possible to digest what I had learned from him and to apply the principles elsewhere in my own way.

Of course one could say that playing like your hero might be possible for a few seconds, but would be impossible to sustain for a few minutes or hours. In reality your hero has unusual reserves of stamina and nerve, accumulated over thousands of hours of practice, which guarantee a high level of playing at all times and not only when adrenalin buoys them up for the length of an amusing demonstration. A brief and vivid effort of imagination by a student, however, can work wonders, especially in a playful context which prevents them from being too cerebral about what they're accomplishing.

Without going so far as to pretend to 'be' someone else, it can be inspiring to encounter a style of playing which resonates with you so much that it feels as though it could be yours too. My husband Bob is a great admirer of the pianist Clifford Curzon. Curzon was a complex kind of role model, because as well as being admired for his meticulous musicianship he was known for his bouts of nerves on the concert stage, nerves which increased as his career developed. His fans suffered with him as they watched his hands actually shaking as he tried to put them down on the keys at the start of a performance. When nerves got the better of him, Curzon was prone to handfuls of wrong notes and memory lapses. None of these spoiled the intrinsic nobility of his piano playing, and indeed his fans developed a remarkable ability to 'see through' the occasional haze of errors to what lay beneath. His distinctive style, a very nuanced and painstaking way of making the piano 'speak' with delicate gradations of touch and timing, struck Bob as an approach which would make perfect sense for his own playing if he could only learn to emulate it. It was a style of playing both new to Bob and yet instantly recognisable because it seemed to come from a kindred musical sensibility. It offered a ready-made model which came from another person and yet felt as though one could have come up with it oneself. It was almost as if Curzon was playing on Bob's behalf.

The Canadian pianist Glenn Gould was another hero for many musicians who might not have enjoyed pretending to be him but identified with his approach. Many people were struck by the rigorous intellectual clarity of Gould's Bach playing, which was like harpsichord playing after a collision with twentieth-century technology. It made people feel there was something very cool about playing Bach in the modern age. Gould retired early from the concert stage in order to devote himself to the recording studio, and his playing is known mainly from his records. So it wasn't his platform manner that people wanted to imitate, perhaps just as well as his posture at the piano – sitting on an extremely low stool and adopting a 'praying mantis' approach to the keyboard – was eccentric. His Bach playing was a refreshing corrective to the fat, heavy, 'important' style then prevalent. His almost machine-like control of individual voices within the music, and the amazing evenness of his fingerwork – which some people thought so unnaturally perfect that it must have been manipulated in post-production – served to show many listeners a new aspect of Bach. (Gould's playing was captured on film, which proves that he could really do it, but more people had heard the recordings than had seen the films.) In a way Gould's playing seemed heartless, but it was undeniably mesmerising. His Bach recordings, particularly his stunning Goldberg Variations, awoke new listeners to the relevance of Bach's music and they happily let their thoughts run along the very particular groove carved out by Gould.

Why don't people play better?

Why don't people play better? That's a question over which many music teachers sigh. Back in the days when violin was my 'second instrument' and I was a member of the violin section of the National Youth Orchestra, our violin coach Hugh Maguire used sometimes to listen to our attempts at playing together, shake his head, search for the right words and then conclude ruefully in his charming Irish brogue, '… Play it better!' We knew what he meant. In a funny way his simple admonition to 'play it better' was helpful, because we hadn't really considered what we sounded like to someone listening from the outside, and to be made aware of it was half the battle.

Even when playing an instrument is meant to be just a fun and delightful pastime, the reasons for 'not playing better' are quite deep and complex. I've often wondered if there is some incentive for people to remain only modestly competent because getting better would carry some undesirable consequences, such as having to practise more, being less available for social activities (especially in the case of teenagers), or becoming in some regrettable way differentiated from other members of one's family or friendship group. As a teacher you sometimes find that someone is just waiting to be pushed to do more, but for the sake of a quiet life many people seem to prefer not to test the boundaries of how good they could be. At any rate, it is safe to say that the reason many people don't play better is not because they can't.

We are all prisoners of the habits we develop while practising the instrument alone. Teachers tell us we should acquire our technique by patient and disciplined practice, building our playing day after day by tiny steps. And of course there are many physical challenges in piano technique which are best approached with an eye to building strength and agility over a long period. But no matter how solid your technique is, using your imagination is equally important for making progress. In fact I'd say that imagination is the prerequisite for becoming a better musician. You can practise and practise, but if you're not constantly wondering what you can *do* with these new skills you're developing, your progress will be lop-sided. The point of practising an instrument is to be able to express more things musically. Scales and arpeggios, for example, are simply designed to make a player feel comfortable and secure when they move about the instrument in any key and at any speed. (Disney's 1970 cartoon film *The Aristocats* had the right idea in its 'Scales and Arpeggios' song when the cats sing that 'Though at first it seems it doesn't show / Like a tree, ability will bloom and grow'.) Yet many beginners experience scales and arpeggios as a purely tedious exercise which puts them off learning the piano. If both teachers and students use a bit of imagination, they can link scales and arpeggios to pieces in which you can feel the benefit of having practised them.

They say that 'a picture is worth a thousand words', and students often find a good image more helpful than a spreadsheet of technical instructions. If you ask a good musician to imagine that, for example, the notes are falling like snow, or that the sound is paper-thin, or that the music is getting dark as they play, they respond with instinctive alteration of their touch and weight on the keyboard. The adjustment is often one that would sound insanely complicated if you tried to analyse it, but if you say, 'Imagine that you are speaking rather than singing', or 'Imagine that you are recalling this from a great distance', people know what to do, more holistically than if you had told them to lean their weight so many degrees this or that way and increase the speed of attack of their fingers on the keys by 37 per cent. Neurologists have told us that when we *imagine* music, the neurons and circuits active in the brain are the same ones active when we are actually hearing music. Encouraging the student to use their imagination is not, therefore, an airy-fairy piece of alternative art therapy or a substitute for actual work. Imagining a musical result is an authentic form of practice, and I wish more people would use this method of practising, which you might say is a musical equivalent of using 'clean energy'.

Once, at the April masterclass course of the International Musicians' Seminar in Prussia Cove, Cornwall, I was playing the piano part of a Brahms cello sonata in a class taught by the wonderful German cello professor Johannes Goritzki. He wanted the piano part to sound bigger and grander. I did my best, but he wasn't hearing what he hoped to hear. The lid of the grand piano was shut at the time. As I continued playing, Goritzki walked over to the piano. With a conspiratorial smile he levered the lid slowly upwards with both hands, as if setting some huge thing in motion. It seemed as though the piano lid was opening in response to something I was doing, as if the air inside the instrument was expanding like a magnificent piano-shaped soufflé, pushing the lid upwards. With a strangely detached feeling I watched Goritzki's antics as I played on, aware that I was being manipulated in the most benevolent way and that the audience was enjoying the theatre of it. The piano part of the Brahms sonata was no less difficult, but instead of focusing exclusively on it, I sat back and let myself watch the lid rising to let more music out. And lo and behold I found myself playing like someone whose playing would cause the piano lid to rise of its own accord. 'Hooray!' said Goritzki, and when I looked round at the class, everyone was smiling. Long afterwards I found that the image of the piano lid slowly rising was enough to bring back a sensation of freedom.

Recent research on how the brain works has suggested that the time we spend daydreaming or 'idling' is probably the equivalent of the hidden but vastly important 'dark matter' in the universe. As we 'mark time' in between tasks, we are digesting experience and visualising the future. When we lie down and rest, our brains may be even more active than when we are at work. Without such periods of 'idling' we are unable to function in a balanced way, yet we don't allot much importance to those periods of mulling things over. Anyone who tries to teach will discover that giving specific tasks may be less effective in the long run than encouraging the student to enter the creative 'mulling space'. As the American neuroscientist Michael Gazzaniga said, 'It's all memory, except for the thin edge of the present.'

Grappling with the instrument

It may seem blindingly obvious to say that musicians should use their imaginations, but many non-musicians don't appreciate how difficult it is for musicians to do so, and for a very important reason: *we are so busy with the task of playing an instrument*. Playing an instrument may seem to the casual observer like a glorious, effortless means of self-expression. Many musicians would endorse the idea that 'play' is a wonderful word for sound-creation and music-making. Yet many musicians would probably also agree that the word 'play' is a misnomer for something that feels so very much like work. The instrument often feels like a recalcitrant lover who has to be conquered anew every day. Oddly enough, an instrument – which is your tool and your means of expression – can even feel like a barrier between you and the music. There is so much to contend with that whole practice sessions and indeed whole years may go by filled with the stubbornly difficult task of mastering a cello, a piano, a French horn or whatever. Grappling with the co-ordination of, say, bow and string, left hand and right hand, or breath and lip, is often as much as a student can deal with at one time. Finding your balance, maintaining your posture, developing accuracy and building up stamina are goals that properly occupy a great deal of time and energy.

I see proof of this all the time in the way that fellow musicians (the ones with portable instruments) practise, practise, practise backstage and in the corridor leading to the stage and sometimes behind the stage door itself until the moment they are called to take their places on the platform. It is as though, even at an advanced level, they are still locked in a struggle for control of the instrument. Technique is not a matter that most musicians can 'take as read' and forget about; many actively keep their technique fresh through daily practice, and would feel remiss if they didn't. Compare this with, for example, the school student in their 'creative writing' lesson. Given that they have learned to read and write (which I realise does not come easily to everyone, but is usually well learned by the time childhood is over), the physical task of creative writing is a straightforward matter of imagining something, putting it into words and writing it down. I am well aware of how difficult it is to have good thoughts and to find good words for them, but in terms of sheer technique, the writer and their notebook are a beautifully simple partnership. Apart from the business of forming the letters on the page, no major technical process has to be negotiated. The imagination does not have to pass through a whole other, external stage before it can be expressed.

I recently belonged to a reading group who met every month to read aloud Homer's *The Iliad* in Robert Fagle's English translation. We did no preparation, but simply took it in turns to read out a few pages. Although none of us knew much about the background of the book, we were all able to get something out of it by 'sight-reading' it. The narrative was evident to us straightaway. I couldn't help comparing this with what would have happened had we met to sight-read, say, all of Beethoven's piano sonatas. Even with a group of competent pianists I could hardly imagine that such a thing could have a happy outcome. In the Homer reading group, the basic text and its meaning were accessible to all of us without a moment's preparation, because we knew how to read and we understood the meaning of words. But in the hypothetical Beethoven sonata group, the text would not have been immediately accessible in the same way. Why not? *Because of the difficulty of playing the piano.* Such a project could only work if each of the pianists had done preparatory work on deciphering the notation, working out the fingering and the physical movements necessary to get around the keyboard, and asking themselves what Beethoven meant by the music. Otherwise, unless we were a group of geniuses, everyone would be condemned to listen to an awful lot of stumbling over wrong notes and mis-reading things, not to mention purely musical blunders. Sight-reading music is much more complex than sight-reading a book, though in both cases it is not straightforward to find the deeper meaning.

As György Sebök observed, 'We could all be wonderful musicians if it weren't for the fact that we have to play instruments.' How marvellous it would be if we could just 'think the music' in our heads and by some magical process make it sound out loud! Perhaps this may be possible one day, now that science has begun to work on 'thought commands' that a person can transmit to a piece of high-tech equipment. We are even starting to hear that one day the contents of a person's brain may be able to be converted into code and uploaded to a computer, to be preserved and utilised by others even after the owner's death. But for now we are still externalising music through the medium of an instrument, and we must learn to play it. Even the human voice, the most immediate of 'instruments', can be remarkably resistant to making the beautiful sounds we hear in our heads. I have music in my head all the time, but when I sing I'm annoyed at how unskilful I sound. I can 'hear' effortless singing but my voice has never been trained, so there is a big gap between what I hear and what I can actually do.

When I was a student I once went along to play the piano for someone's singing lesson. The singer was having trouble reaching a certain high note without looking and sounding strained. Her teacher made a couple of suggestions about relaxing the throat, supporting from the diaphragm and so on. She tried again, but the high note still came out as an effortful squeak. Then her teacher said, 'Imagine that you have just sung a note a whole octave above the one you're trying to reach.' (The student closed her eyes and imagined it. It was a note too high for anyone to sing in reality.) 'Now you are going to glide *down* from that super-high note, down, down until you land gently on the note we want. It will seem easy in comparison!' Still with her eyes closed, the singer imagined the stratospherically high note and you could see her adjusting her throat as she imagined gliding down an octave to the note we were after. She opened her mouth and sung it with no strain. The teacher and I both applauded. I was enthralled. Never had I seen such an effective 'trick'. I knew that, even if the trick didn't work a second time, the singer would retain some physical memory of singing the high note without strain. Rather than trying to remember a series of technical instructions, she could now imagine how pleasant it was to sing a high note when you 'had just been singing one an octave higher'.

In many other arts, such as painting or sculpture, the artist has to master technical issues, but I rather doubt whether any art presents such formidable challenges as that of mastering a musical instrument to play classical repertoire, which I single out because of its complexities of expressivity, notation and structure. Even a competent player with a good idea of the result they want to achieve may find it frustratingly difficult to translate their vision into reality once the instrument is in their hands. It is no surprise then that so many teachers have to spend a large amount of lesson time drawing students' attention to the composer's markings and to the artistic effect they're aiming at; these matters are often banished to the back of the student's mind as they grapple with the task of simply getting round the instrument with decent tone and tuning.

There's a famous story about Beethoven's friend, the violinist Ignaz Schuppanzigh, complaining to him about the difficulty of some of the writing for the first violin in the opus 59 string quartets. Beethoven is said to have replied, 'When the spirit speaks to me, do you think it speaks in terms of your wretched instrument?' His remark showed how much he took it for granted that his mission was to express his spirit and personality through music, not to provide something that he knew would lie pleasantly under the musicians' hands. Although Beethoven wanted his music to be played, it was not his *primary* aim to provide music that was easily playable (and as such, he probably represents a new era in the self-definition of The Composer). When I think of Beethoven's words to Schuppanzigh, I feel that many players grappling with the difficult violin parts might burst out crossly: 'Do you think, when I am dealing with this wretched instrument, that I can hear your spirit speaking to me?'

Many more books have been written about instrumental technique than about what to do with it once you have it. Technique should always be a means to an end, but there are many – both players and listeners – who seem to feel that if the technique is impressive in its own right, why not flaunt it? In every generation there are performers who have made a career out of having great technique, even if it is not musically apparent what they want to have a great technique *for*. (As Sándor Végh once observed to a very accomplished violinist I was playing with, 'You have a very good technique, but you don't know what to do with it. You are like a millionaire. You have a lot of money, but no idea what to spend it on.') Playing the notes fast, accurately and brilliantly becomes a sporting endeavour which celebrates strength, speed and co-ordination. Even if you pursue only these qualities, there's a lot to get right, and for quite a few people those aims appear to be sufficient. I was once startled to hear a very fine player describe his approach to mastering a piece in these terms: 'I work out the fingering and the bowing. I work out how to get from note to note securely, with good tone. I work out how to play in tune. I pay attention to the louds and softs. That's all there is to it.' Anything beyond that, he once said, amounted to 'making up stuff to worry about'. His audiences may not have felt deeply moved, but they were enthusiastic about his secure, unfussy playing. I suspected that they liked his style partly because it made them feel that classical music was more straightforward than they had thought. I used to wonder secretly whether this no-nonsense practical approach to being a musician would last him a lifetime, and indeed as time went by I believe his interest moved elsewhere.

Words and signs

My visits to the homes of composers – Mozart, Haydn, Beethoven, Ravel, Grieg, Elgar, for example – made me aware of the labour involved in writing down music in a pre-technological age. Seeing the quill pens, the paper, the reading glasses, the inkpots, the lack of decent lighting and so on made me realise how arduous it was to produce a musical score, particularly one with many parts. Just imagine the labour involved in the days when you had to begin by ruling lines on paper or parchment to produce musical staves! Ruling long lines with a nib and ink is not an easy matter, as I remember from the days when all my school work was done with an Osmiroid pen, an italic nib and a bottle of ink which one would sometimes knock over accidentally onto the desk with one's elbow, ruining the work. As a student I had some experience in writing down music for weekly 'harmony and counterpoint' exercises. Occasionally I had to write out instrumental parts for rehearsals. I knew how painstaking it was to write all the rhythms with their single, double, triple-barring across the stems of notes, the rests with their various shapes, the dots which prolonged the duration of a note but mustn't look like a note-head, and the notes themselves which if carelessly written might seem to be 'on the line' instead of 'in the space' or vice versa. I knew from my experience of playing the violin that a poorly-written orchestral part with ambiguous note-heads would cause players to make mistakes and waste time in rehearsals. I began to have a sense of the gap between the time it took to conceive of a musical phrase or piece, and the time it took to write it down. I could imagine how exasperating it was for composers to have to hold the musical thought in their heads, trying not to let it disappear as they dissected it into the hundreds of pitches and rhythms necessary to 'make them real', with intricate strokes of the pen to delineate them all. Clearly, nobody would bother unless they had great faith in the importance of what they were notating.

By contrast, I also had plenty of experience of creative writing of poetry and imaginative essays, and I knew how long that took. The *writing down* was a simple task. I became sensitive to the labour involved in writing down famous musical themes as opposed to famous lines of poetry or theatre plays. Take the opening of Mozart's *Marriage of Figaro*, for example, the opening of Beethoven's Fifth Symphony, or of Handel's 'Hallelujah Chorus'. Twenty seconds of music in orchestral and vocal score probably took an hour to write down. Compare this with a Shakespeare sonnet, an Edward Lear limerick, or a haiku by Basho. Naturally the lines themselves may have taken a long time to think up and refine, but to *write down* the literary line was the work of a few seconds, whereas the notating of the musical phrase was almost an artwork in itself.

These experiences have trained me to do 'close reading' of notation. I often find that if I follow all the composer's markings (for example, being accurate about phrase-marks, rests and words indicating degrees of loud and soft), a more interesting and complicated result emerges – surprising for some people who are used to 'the usual way of playing it' but closer, I hope, to the one the composer wanted. One of the things that has surprised me as a teacher is that many people seem to treat aspects of notation rather as they would treat the small print on a contract, which is to say they don't bother to pay attention to it as long as they have grasped the basic idea of how things go. It's as if they glance at the score for long enough to figure out what notes they are to play, but then divert their attention to looking at their hands on the keyboard, and forget to look back to check what other markings there are in the score. Their aim is to feel freer, but *musically* the neglect of the composer's markings usually results in a blunter and blander effect. I find I'm constantly pointing out to people that they haven't noticed this or that in the score, and they almost always admit that indeed they hadn't noticed it. They admit it rather nonchalantly, as though they had assumed the composer was just killing time when they went to the trouble of writing in slurs, rests, dynamic changes and so on. Yet when they look more closely and remedy the oversight, they are usually pleased with the result. This has made me realise that how we use or don't use notation is a complicated subject. Notation is our primary source of knowledge about what the composer meant, yet we resist it. We need it in order to learn anything too complex to be learned by ear, but it seems that there is only so much of a player's mind that can be spared for notation when they're absorbed in playing their instrument.

In music, there is a huge vocabulary of words and signs that give us information about the mood, the tempo, the touch, the phrasing, the loud and soft, the speeding up and slowing down, the heavy and light, and the changes of mood that occur during the piece. In literature there is nothing equivalent except for stage directions, which are nothing like as detailed as musical annotations. The 'tone' of a line of poetry or a piece of drama is famously ambiguous and open to many interpretations. People complain that it is very difficult to interpret the tone of an email or a text message; that they thought something was serious when it was really lighthearted, abrupt when it was just meant to be brief, or hurtful when it was meant ironically. Such errors of interpretation are less likely to happen in notated music where there are usually clues if not detailed instructions about the 'tone'. I often think that writers could usefully learn from composers how to signal tone and timing, though of course if they did, it would complicate the process of literary notation immensely. Opponents of the change would complain that only 'the elite' would feel comfortable with reading books, a charge that is often levelled against music notation.

Although music notation is full of clues and instructions, there is still an enormous amount that is not notated and would not be possible to notate without making the score look like a mathematical working-out. For example, I have never come across any way of indicating exactly what a 'crescendo' means. Crescendo is one of the signs encountered in almost every piece of music. It means 'growing', usually taken to mean 'getting louder' or 'growing in loudness', but how much? Should it get just a few degrees louder, or many degrees louder? Should it get louder at a constant rate, or should the curve be calibrated so that most of the 'growing' happens towards the end of the passage marked 'crescendo'? Should it be just a little crescendo, a subset of whatever is the prevailing marking, for example 'piano', meaning soft? Sándor Végh sometimes called such a thing 'a crescendo within piano', meaning that although the music was to get louder, it was not to stray outside the confines of 'quiet'. Or might it be one of those crescendos which doesn't mean 'getting louder' but actually means 'growing' in another sense, such as growing in expression? To represent exactly what the composer had in mind with any particular crescendo there would probably need to be a sign expressing gradient. Since there is no such convention, musicians tend to have a sort of Pavlovian response to the crescendo sign, increasing the loudness in a predictable way not always derived from the musical context.

The same is true of markings like diminuendo (getting softer, diminishing), 'staccato' (detached), or the frequently encountered but rarely defined marking for a 'pause'. What is the meaning of the pause? How long should one pause for? Is the pause related to the prevailing tempo? How many extra beats should one incorporate into a pause? Is it important that the length of the pause be guessable or unguessable? I generally find that people make pauses too long, but that may simply reflect my tendency to be impatient. Many people seem to have been told by their music teachers to double the length of the note with a 'pause' written above it. In fact, a pause almost always has some kind of rhetorical effect or emotional meaning; its silence needs careful handling so that the music doesn't become empty during the pause. The length of the pause and the player's body language during the pause have to be derived from the musical context; it is not helpful to tell students simply to apply a standard multiple to the length of the note with a pause sign over it.

How to notate the use of pedal on the piano is another minefield. Many of my students have noticed that how composers notate the pedal is not strictly logical. For example, they often indicate where the sustaining pedal is to be pressed down, but not where it is to be lifted; that is left to the wit of the pianist, and though the answer is sometimes obvious, it isn't always. If there is a move to another key, a change of harmony, or the arrival of a new theme, a player will usually understand that the sound mustn't be blurred, but even here there are exceptions, because blurring can be meaningful. Composers often indicate where they particularly *want* the effect of the pedal being held down, but we are unwise to think that therefore they didn't expect it to be used anywhere else; they were probably just highlighting special places where the use of the pedal was non-negotiable. More problematically, notation often indicates that while the sustaining pedal is being held down, the pianist should play certain notes staccato or short. But if the pedal is down when they do so, the notes will ring on, and will sound long. What then did composers mean? I've come to think that such markings refer to what the performer must *do*, rather than how it sounds. Creating a musical performance, or watching and listening to one, is a multi-sensory experience and when a pianist plays short notes through a haze of pedal, the audio-visual effect has its own point.

Tempo is character

Tempo instructions, by convention often in Italian, present similar problems. For a start, they are often ignored. I've lost count of the number of times I've asked a student, 'Why are you playing it so slowly? The marking is andante', or the opposite: 'Why are you playing it so fast? The marking is moderato', and so on. Students often look up at the score with surprise, notice the marking as if for the first time, and say, 'Oh yes, so it is! I hadn't realised.' When I try to find out why they are playing at a different tempo than the one requested by the composer, they usually say something like, 'Because I'm used to hearing it like that on the record'. Aural tradition is important in its own way; if a person has liked a piece on hearing it played in a certain way, one can understand why they might unconsciously copy it, but I'm not sure I have ever encountered a student who clings to their 'old way' once we have registered the original tempo instruction and explored what the composer must have meant by it.

Tempo instructions are often indications as much of character as of speed. For example, 'andante' means 'going along', not 'moderately slow' as it is often translated. 'Allegro' means 'merry' or 'cheerful', not just 'at a brisk tempo'. 'Adagio' literally means 'at ease' or 'leisurely', not 'very slow'. Custom and use, not to mention grade exams which supply standard 'meanings' of these words, have oversimplified them but it is as well to be reminded that in a very important sense, tempo *is* character. When a composer uses a word like 'vivace' at the start, it signifies liveliness as well as a quick tempo. But the character and speed indicated at the beginning of the piece may not be relevant to every part of it. There may be a single word such as 'allegro' at the beginning, but this instruction may only apply to the opening section of the piece, and the first time there is a change of mood with no further marking you must decide whether to adjust the tempo accordingly. Perhaps a tempo heading at the start of the piece is a little like a chapter heading in a novel, 'Mr Pickwick in chase of his hat', say, or 'An extraordinary scene between Sophie and her Aunt', but as we know from reading, there may be many pages of the chapter which are nothing at all to do with the heading.

The composer may give a single instruction of 'forte' or 'piano', but nothing else for bars and bars, even pages. Within a 'forte' section many shades of loudness may be needed to express the music. Assertive loud, secure loud, defiant loud, triumphant loud? One might go as far as the great cellist Pablo Casals who commented that 'within every forte there is a piano, and within every piano there is a forte'. Such a statement may sound nonsensical, but since music is a living process, a change from soft to loud or vice versa contains (and often expresses) the potential to grow afresh, or to diminish again. Then there are all the words which indicate speeding up and slowing down – accelerando and ritardando for example. As with crescendo markings, there is no simple way to indicate the degree of speeding up or slowing down except by adding a word like 'poco' (a little) or 'molto' (a lot), which still leaves the performer with plenty of decisions to make. Composers have traditionally, and understandably, been reluctant to overload the score with instructions apart from the notes. (Edward Elgar observed that the more instructions he gave, the more it seemed to confuse the musicians.) Thus, even though a player is given the broad brushstroke of 'allegro' or 'andante' or 'vivace' as an indication of prevailing character, they are still faced with making hundreds of tiny adjustments too fleeting to be notated, yet essential to the life of the piece.

Notation gives us a clue about how to perform 'ornaments' such as trills, turns, mordents and little flights of fancy written in a font size tinier than the usual. By making them so small, the composer seems to me to be signalling that the ornaments or little decorative passages must be relatively light or fleeting compared with the notes around them. Yet ornaments often require intricate fingering patterns, and people often play them in an effortful, lumpy way which makes them stick out of the melody line. At Piano Club one day it occurred to me to say that ornaments are meant to be tiny, sparkling things that make something more beautiful, like a glittering earring or a jewel in the hair. This visual image proved much more effective than giving technical advice. The person who was playing smiled and immediately adjusted their way of playing so that the ornament was no longer a rattle of gunfire but a little spray of perfume, which fitted perfectly into the style of the music. I recently attended a concert by the Italian jazz pianist Rossano Sportiello, who included a couple of Chopin mazurkas (un-jazzed-up) in his programme. His way of playing Chopin's little ornaments and cadenzas was a model of how to do it, and this was linked to his experience as an improviser, making everything sound as if it had just occurred to him.

Early in my acquaintance with the Hungarian violinist Sándor Végh, at the Prussia Cove spring seminar, I was playing one day for a violinist's lesson on the Beethoven C minor Sonata for piano and violin. We had arrived at the slow movement, which the piano begins on its own with a particularly beautiful melodic paragraph. I was about to play it, when Végh motioned to me to wait.

'I was once playing this on a concert tour with Wilhelm Kempff,' he said to the assembled listeners, 'and we got to the next town. I was tired and hungry. I was fed up with being away from home. I didn't feel like rehearsing, but the pianist wanted to. My thoughts were far away. And then Kempff started this movement.' (Végh paused and opened his eyes widely to denote amazement.) 'He played it *so beautifully* that all my feelings of tiredness just disappeared. I felt completely fresh. Everything was all right again.' Without bringing down the curtain on this lovely picture he leaned forward and motioned for me to play, like a director summoning his lead actor. I could easily have tensed up, but he had put me on the spot with no time to think, and all I could do was try to evoke the scene. I tried to 'be' that skilful pianist, to feel a sense of calm and expansiveness. It's important to say that I tried to 'be' it without acting. And maybe I succeeded, or perhaps the listeners were tricked into hearing it, but Végh settled back in his big carved chair, listening to me with a beatific smile. I don't know what I did in technical terms, but the thought of being able to make someone forget their hunger and fatigue was very inspiring. It was more helpful than being told to play more slowly or quietly, or to let the rests resonate for longer. I possibly did all those things, as a matter of fact, but I didn't subdivide my guiding principle into dozens of little tasks. I just thought 'make them forget that they are tired' and let my musicianship take over. It was a good experience which gave me a newfound sense of expressive possibility. What it taught me was that, given a strong and overarching image or emotion as a guide, one can synthesise the many technical elements needed to achieve it without even being conscious of them as individual tasks.

In my Piano Club I am often struck by how strongly the music comes across if someone really understands its character and wants me to understand it too. We all agree that the spirit of the music can survive remarkably unimpaired by things like wrong notes, missing notes, uneven fingerwork and so on. We have people who are not technically advanced, or perhaps not confident as performers, but whose grasp of musical mood and character is so strong that the message comes across loud and clear. The Germans have a wonderful word, 'Ausstrahlung' (shining-out, radiance, aura), which comes to my mind at such moments and I marvel at how the deeper meaning can be evident despite all manner of superficial impediments and flaws.

Connecting the beats

At the start of this section I mentioned a pianist who made heavy
weather of a piece by 'marking time' through the individual beats,
making it very plain that he was counting them inwardly. He isn't
alone in doing this; many people seem to think that it proves their
musicality if they show they know where the beats are. There are
some types of music – dance music for example – where thumping
out the beats has a practical point and is an essential part of the
style. In many types of folk and pop music the individual beats are
there to be enjoyed with toe-tapping, stamping the foot, slapping
the knee and so on. Somehow, stamping out the beats gives its own
energy, and this is brought to a tremendous pitch by an art form like
flamenco. But in classical music, as in classical ballet, the aim is to
create a sense of longer flow in which the beats are dropped down
to a lower level of importance for the sake of creating a musical
phrase, a story, an atmosphere. Energy should move irresistibly along
the chain of individual notes, and for that to happen, the beats have
to be minimised. In both ballet and classical music the aim is often
to 'rise up' against the pull of gravity. This is probably why it feels so
odd when a famous classical piece is 'modernised' by having a 'click
track' or drum beat added to it. It's supposed to make the music

more accessible but, for me at least, adding a rhythm track only fixes the attention on individual beats. 'Updating' classical music in this way makes it not simpler, but cruder.

The whole art of such music is to connect, and by connecting to create long spans and structures that support time in a special way. In 1989 the French classical ballerina Yvette Chauviré spoke about changes she had observed in ballet technique, lamenting that 'ballet had become hi-tech'. 'They exploit jumps or certain beats, or pirouettes, or those stretches that go on for ever, but they have forgotten that dance is made up of directions and *épaulements [rotations of the shoulders and head in ballet]*. I find that at the moment, people have difficulty making the head, the arms and the torso relate to what the legs are doing, how that all fits together', she was quoted as saying. 'For example, in a jump, I see people going up like rockets, in one blow, BAM! Losing what should be the value of each successive moment, rising, and then ending when one touches the ground. Instead, they're suddenly up in the air and it just stops right there, and the whole singing quality is lost' (quoted in her obituary in *The Guardian*, 20 October 2016). 'The whole singing quality' was a wonderful metaphor to use about ballet. I knew exactly what she meant, because piano teachers talk all the time about 'singing', even though pianists don't use their voices in performance any more than ballet dancers do. 'Singing' is a lovely way to convey the idea that notes are carried forward on a single breath, *the connection between the notes* (or movements, in the case of dance) being of the essence.

I pointed out to an amateur pianist who came for a lesson that she was accenting every beat. She was taken aback. 'You *don't* want me to accent every beat?' she asked in all innocence. 'I thought you were meant to?' 'No, I don't want you to', I told her. 'The beats are there anyway. We can't help hearing them. What we want to do is *to rise above* the beats, looking for the musical line.' This simple piece of advice would seem obvious if we were talking about the written word. When you point out to people that they would never accent every 'beat' as they read out a favourite poem such as Wordsworth's

'Daffodils' (e.g. 'I WANDered LONEly AS a CLOUD that FLOATS on HIGH o'er VALES and HILLS'), they smile at the nonsensical effect. We are all so close to words and speech that we naturally understand how individual words act to convey thoughts across a sentence. Yet we seem to find it difficult to adopt the same approach to music. When they play music, many people do the equivalent of stressing every beat in a line of poetry, not realising that by stressing every beat they are preventing the music from taking wing.

Sometimes when I'm trying to explain the idea of long, floating phrases, I find it useful to use the metaphor of flying. If I ask people to imagine flying through the music, they instinctively take away the emphasis from individual beats. They lighten their touch and, as they imagine themselves rising up in the air, they also imagine seeing further. This usually has a remarkable effect on their playing. Their phrases become longer, and their telling of the musical story starts to proceed in whole 'sentences' or 'paragraphs' rather than notes or beats. In such cases it is the student who is 'doing the work', but suddenly it does not feel like work. In fact, people quite often mention that the sensation of 'flying' through the music reminds them of how they can 'fly' in their dreams.

When I was studying in America I had a friend who had no experience of classical music but was a big fan of Elvis and of 'country and western' music. I was studying jazz at the time, and one day I tried to describe my frustration with a student jazz group whose idea of 'hard swing' was to accentuate every beat. I said I'd been trying to get them to play the beats with a shallower bounce, so that the listener's mind was drawn instead to the onward flow of the musical phrase. I did a demonstration of the two contrasting styles. My country-and-western-loving friend was captivated in a way I wasn't used to achieving when I talked about phrasing. 'Do that again!' he said. 'I don't understand what you just did!' I did it again, explaining the difference. He was charmed. 'I never knew you could actually *decide* not to make the beats so heavy,' he said. 'I thought beats **had** to be heavy. I thought music was basically the enjoyment of heavy beats. You've just shown me that you have a choice! That's fantastic! I'm going to listen to things in a different way now.' It was probably one of my most successful pedagogical illustrations ever. But it also made me feel sad that he had never come across any musical style in which the beats were not thumped out.

Sensing the style

We hear a lot these days about the importance of 'originality'. Judges in televised competitions for cookery, painting or pottery are often heard exhorting competitors to 'be original'. I have mixed feelings about this because it doesn't seem to me that 'originality' should be a primary goal. It may turn out that something you have done *is* original, but originality should be a by-product. Telling people to 'be original' usually seems to result in their dreaming something up 'just to be different'.

In classical music, where the notes are given to us, performers sometimes express originality by adding performance effects. Sometimes these illuminate the content of the music, but often they are a kind of meta-narrative with a visual purpose, such as emphasising the performer's looks. Swaying from side to side, tossing their hair, looking fierce, raising their eyes to the ceiling, 'dancing' on the platform, playing theatrically loud or soft – these are all designed to draw attention to the *performer* rather than to the music. In the world of the theatre there's a word for this kind of acting: 'ham'. I saw it recently in a televised concert where a young violinist was all but snorting and pawing the ground in a piece of music which (to my ear) didn't in any way call for that kind of behaviour. I realised I was seeing a sort of 'hamming', an over-acting done for the benefit of the cameras. Does it matter? We live in an image-conscious society. It worries me because I feel that if visuals become the dominant strand of a performance, music will become a supplementary effect, just as it is in movies. We may lose our ability to understand music as a primary language.

Musicians should be encouraged to develop an acute sensitivity to the sonorities, textures and rhythms of music as well as to the mentality of the composer. It helps to have awareness of historical style and, perhaps, some knowledge of the country or nationality concerned because this often gives such a special flavour to music. Did the composer look out of their window at endless forests or lakes? Did they hear people's voices ringing in the frozen winter air? Was their music affected by having to compose quietly in order not to disturb the neighbours who lived in flats around them? Were they in exile, remembering a warmer, more colourful homeland? Does their music flow naturally from them, or is it marked by reluctance or struggle? Are they trying to express something more than they actually do express? Do they aim to transcend their personal problems, or to give voice to them? Did they write music in order to console, or in order to escape, or perhaps to deliver a polemical message? Is it music which needs an audience?

When understanding the style of a piece of music, particularly from a distant era or place, it's very important to understand that although its language may seem to us like 'a style', it was not *a style* for the person who created it and their contemporaries who played it and listened to it. It was merely the way they expressed themselves at the time. Only we, who view it through the lens of another culture or historical period, treat it as something slightly foreign to us, an archaic language or dialect we must try to learn. The great art of playing in any style is to find a way to identify with the language and make it feel like an absolutely natural way to express music. Our aim should be to make the audience forget they are hearing 'Italian Baroque' or 'German Romanticism' and simply hear direct musical communication. This sounds simple but is not simple in practice, because it means finding your way into the mindset of the people who found it completely natural to shape music in that way. Some musicians appear to be able to do this quite easily, while others achieve it with the help of study, and still others never transcend the boundaries of style at all and always seem a little stilted when they play works of a historical period. It's a very intriguing challenge and so satisfying when one can find a way to meet it.

When musicians spend a lot of time with a work of music, they develop an almost synaesthetic understanding of it, by which I mean that they begin to 'see' and 'feel' it and sometimes to experience it as symbolising relationships and situations. I've often thought that scientists would be intrigued to hear the language that musicians use in rehearsal when they feel safe to express their feelings about the music without fear of ridicule. The imagery they use is drawn from a wide spectrum of non-musical subjects such as food, fabric and texture, colour, smell, weight, pressure and so on. Some might say that 'it feels as if a shadow is passing over the music', or that 'this feels like a story we are telling against our will'. They might say, 'now we need to turn the temperature up', or 'it needs to become light here and float away'. People often speak about the music 'going into the distance' or 'coming towards us'. They talk about the music 'going down the stairs' or 'opening a window'. They talk about 'cooking' or 'baking' the music in rehearsal. They often use nature images such as the sun coming out, the wind blowing, darkness falling, flowers opening. These images are not plucked randomly from the musicians' imaginations; they are synaesthetic responses, and no doubt if we could look inside their heads we would see the neurological equivalent of 'sympathetic strings'. Not everyone relates to music like this, but I think I could say that all my close musical colleagues do. In fact, everyone seems to have a degree of synaesthetic response to music. In Piano Club we have had fun discussing 'what colour' different keys are. Obviously there is no rational way to link keys to colours, but it is surprising how readily people agree that G major 'is green' or that A major 'is red'.

Many words indicating character and mood need a little unpacking. At a recent meeting of my Piano Club, we discussed how to interpret the instruction 'maestoso' (majestic), a frequent expression marking in eighteenth- and nineteenth-century classical music. Perhaps in Handel's or Mozart's time 'maestoso' would have been easily understood, but it now seems to have moved into the realm of historical images which need some explanation. Clifford Curzon quoted Artur Schnabel as having said that it is wrong to interpret 'maestoso' as something slow and laborious (and indeed this is borne out by the number of times that one comes across a pairing of words like 'allegro maestoso' – lively and majestic – in the music of Handel, Bach, Haydn, Mozart, Beethoven, and even Chopin and Liszt in the nineteenth century). To give an impression of majesty it is important to seem effortless, as though the laws of gravity don't apply to you. A king or queen should sail lightly through the palace, never weighed down by the cares of state but rather floating above them through divine elevation. This image had a remarkable effect on the person who had just plodded slowly through a 'majestic' piece. She turned back to the piano and we could all see that in her mind she was a weightless monarch. She set off again with a faster, lighter tempo and a more joyful character. Even her facial expression conveyed a change of attitude, and the enthusiastic response of all the listeners let her know she had hit on something important.

We have also pondered what composers mean when they use the word 'espressivo'. Musical dictionaries are of little help, usually stating that 'a passage marked "espressivo" is to be played expressively', implying that there is some other kind of musical passage *not* to be played expressively. Admittedly it seems unhelpful of composers simply to use the word 'espressivo', as if a cook were to pass down an old recipe with the instruction, 'Add flavourings'. If composers have a specific expression in mind, why not write 'sadly' or 'cheerfully' or 'dreamily'? Or could it be that when a composer writes 'espressivo' they are just giving permission for the player to take some liberties with the timing and dynamics? Again, the precise meaning of the term as Haydn or Chopin might have used it is lost to us. They certainly did not mean that *only* a passage marked 'espressivo' is to be played with expression. My feeling is that they probably meant 'if you are a good musician you will know what special flavour to give this passage'. But special flavours come in many varieties and I am sure they didn't mean that every 'espressivo' passage is to be played in the same way, using a generalised romantic lingering, as tends to happen nowadays.

So, having said what 'espressivo' *isn't*, what is it? Usually it seems to me that 'espressivo' appears when there is a momentary change in the flow or the type of information. Perhaps the texture of the music suddenly becomes more dense, or there is more emotional charge in the melodic line, indicated by wider intervals or more pressure of notes. Or the music may suddenly stop being busy and become slow, thin and sad. Perhaps there are new harmonies in the bass, bringing a sense of changing character. Maybe the prevailing 'soft' or 'loud' is interrupted by an urgent expression of another kind which is not to be summed up in a simple instruction, but has to be felt. Behind the rather bland façade of an instruction like 'espressivo', one senses a background in which composer and player belonged to the same culture and the same era, such that a composer could rely on a player to share his understanding of taste, manners and nuances of expression. A composer writing 'with expression' for a contemporary wouldn't have to worry that they might do something wildly inappropriate in response. As time goes by, however, and we may be centuries distant from the composer, the meaning of 'espressivo' can fade like an old photograph.

The same applies to all those places in the music where it might seem natural, for example, to slow up before or relax the tempo at the appearance of a big new melody, or at a significant change to a new key. Some composers give an instruction, such as 'ritardando' or 'allargando' (slowing down, broadening out) at such places. Many give no guidance at all. Does this mean that nothing is to be done? Again, the lack of specific instruction probably means the composer took it for granted that any good musician could be trusted to do the appropriate thing without being told how. I remember a long argument between members of an international group in a rehearsal of a Schubert 'minuet and trio' where half the group felt it was obvious that the 'trio' section should relax in tempo (partly because the music was simpler), while the other half felt that because the composer had not written a new tempo instruction at that point, it was our duty *not to slow down*. It struck me that the musicians who felt we should naturally take a slower tempo were the Austrians. When they said '*of course* we slow down for this section', they had no logic on their side, but they were bathed in the performance tradition in which Schubert himself lived, and that gave their words a special weight.

But when we try to analyse the composer's silence, we are in danger of finding ourselves in the surreal world of American humorist James Thurber, who in his 1950 essay, 'What Cocktail Party?', memorably describes what the guests at a cocktail party think T.S. Eliot means or does not mean when he fails to say things in his play, *The Cocktail Party*. Stumped by a question about what Eliot does not mean, Thurber plays for time by asking his interlocutor, 'Do you mean what Eliot is *intentionally* not saying, or what he just *happens* not to have said?' In music the composer's intentions can be similarly inscrutable. It poses a problem for the teacher who is trying to train students not to invent things or overlay the composer's wishes with their own. Sometimes we tell them that they are not to change tempo or mood if the composer doesn't indicate it. Sometimes we tell them that although the composer hasn't indicated as much, it is musically obvious that an adjustment is needed. The difference between the two is subtle. I could always give *musical* reasons for saying one or the other, but naturally it has taken long acquaintance with the repertoire and a good deal of background reading for me to develop my sense of what is appropriate, and as the learner has not yet had that long acquaintance it is up to me to mediate between the composer and the modern performer.

Imagery, positive and negative

My Piano Club is a small and homely version of a masterclass, where students gather to listen to one another's lessons and take it in turns to play in front of the whole class. Such a forum is an excellent basis for sharing and collective learning, and is economical for the tutor, who does not have to re-state important principles at every lesson, because everyone heard them the first time and (at least in theory) can apply them in other contexts. The public setting, however, tends to make every judgement seem larger and more dramatic than it might be in an individual lesson. Traditionally a student is not invited to challenge a master's pronouncements, and while some 'masters' are sensitive to this one-sided situation, others exploit it.

Just as a well-chosen positive image can enable a student to excel themselves, a negative one can set them back with long-lasting effect. Some years ago at a public masterclass in London I heard a highly-regarded Eastern European professor tell a student that when they played they were 'like a Bolshevik, lining the notes up in front of them and then shooting them one by one'. (He mimed the scene, narrowing his eyes as he took aim at the poor unfortunate notes.) 'And the notes cannot care – because they are all dead', he finished with a flourish. The audience gasped with horror, or was it ghoulish enjoyment? At any rate I doubt whether the student ever forgot being told that they were murdering notes, and it would be a rare person who was able to turn such a provocation into educational gold. It's one of the drawbacks of public masterclasses that the student has no obvious right of reply, and who would have the presence of mind to reply to something so devastating? It is this kind of behaviour that leads some disillusioned people to regard masterclasses as 'hit and run' teaching, where a visiting tutor bursts into the student's life in a blaze of irresponsible metaphor and then vanishes, leaving the regular teacher to pick up the pieces and help the student sort out what was worth learning and what should be speedily forgotten.

Masterclasses are a way of teaching which I didn't encounter until I was already finished with university. I later discovered that they were a respected method of teaching in mainland Europe, which gradually spread to many UK educational institutions and courses. When I first experienced masterclasses, at the International Musicians' Seminar in Prussia Cove, I was immediately impressed with the good sense of teaching a roomful of attentive students at the same time and in front of one another. It is the bane of many music teachers' lives that general principles have to be stated over and over again at individual lessons because only one student at a time ever hears them. In a masterclass, everyone heard whatever wise or helpful remark was made. If the principle was indeed re-stated at many lessons, it was because it was really important, and the re-statement added to its stature. I had not anticipated the fascination of observing other people's lessons. No matter how advanced they were, there was something to learn, even from watching how they responded to advice. It was almost like having a lesson yourself; in fact it was sometimes even better, because you could just focus on what was happening without being distracted by nerves, which as everyone knows can make you deaf to what is being said to you. When it was my turn to play in the class, I immediately realised how painful it was to be criticised in front of everyone, but at the same time I also found what a 'high' it gave me to be praised with all my fellow students listening. Everything, including words of wisdom, seemed to be magnified by the setting.

A masterclass is usually taught by someone special, someone the students admire, someone with enormous performing experience and the credibility that experience confers. Many music teachers don't have a lot of high-level performing experience and it is invaluable to play to someone who does, because their angle of view may be quite different; for example, they may be less concerned with classic technique and more with communicative potential. A visiting teacher, however, may only hear a student once and never again. Their task is very different from that of the 'regular' teacher who has to guide the student through weekly lessons and keep them on an even keel. With luck, a good masterclass professor will be able to see the student in perspective. They may be able to give, and they often do give, nuggets of advice which provoke sudden insights. Masterclass professors are not constrained by knowing what those routine weekly lessons are concerned with and what the usual topics of discussion are. In a masterclass, the 'master' can say whatever seems important to say, even if the student's regular teacher might have been trying not to say it, had never thought of saying it, or would be furious with the visiting tutor for saying it. The potential problem lies in the fact that the 'master' doesn't have to pick up the pieces after a masterclass. They can take risks and say things which *may* be instantly helpful, but might also be deeply unsettling and even destructive. In my own experience, the helpful things said in masterclasses have far outweighed the unhelpful, but not all of my colleagues or students would agree with me. Public masterclasses are in their own way a performance arena, and often seem to tempt the visiting teacher to 'play to the gallery'.

As a masterclass student I've been on the receiving end of some remarks of dubious educational value: 'You play everything as a blonde', the Hungarian cellist János Starker once told me disdainfully, as though blondes were clones who played everything identically. I suppose he was suggesting that my playing seemed elegant and restrained, like the ice-cool blondes of the movies; 'blonde' was a cheap metaphor which may have amused the audience, but didn't really help me. 'Don't be so *British*' was another rebuke he made when I was playing to him with my group Domus, again presupposing that all British people have the same qualities (even a passing acquaintance with the rest of my group would have shown that this was not the case). 'Being British' meant, I suppose, that I was understating things, concealing my true feelings from the audience. But one person's understatement is another person's statement, and statements are understood in very different ways in different cultures. I find this when rehearsing with musicians from different countries. Although I often feel I have stated my wishes in no uncertain terms, it can turn out that my mode of expression ('British understatement') has been perceived as the merest hint, not a definite statement of needs. The same can be true in terms of musical expression. People have deeply ingrained 'learned' parameters of good and bad taste, over-expression and under-expression. Someone from a culture of understatement may play in a way that feels passionate or committed *to them* and be perfectly understood as such by a fellow countryman. It can come as a shock to be told by someone from another culture that you are doing no more than hinting at the emotions contained in the music. It works the other way round as well. A melodramatic piece of 'overstatement' can be offensive to someone from a culture which prizes reticence. It's good to try to see yourself through other eyes, but painful to be accused of 'not saying what you mean' if you *are* actually saying what you mean.

When I was a postgraduate student taking part in international masterclasses, I witnessed a good many 'theatrical' lessons. They were often effective, sometimes even moving, but I also felt that there were too many shock tactics being employed. I came to dislike the public lesson from which the student emerged in tears to be comforted by their friends. It was, and still is, a source of wonder to me how quickly the humiliated student would start saying that it was 'good for them' to have a shock like that. When I started teaching, I vowed never to use such tactics myself. I hadn't liked seeing them used on others. I disliked seeing the victims go into contortions to rationalise the experience. I had delved a little into Alice Miller's psychology books, and I could imagine all too easily that a student who had 'survived' being insulted and 'profited from the experience' would go on to insult their own students in turn.

In any case, and no matter whether this is fair or not, I have never felt it was productive for female professors to use shock tactics. Although students often seem to be stoical about a certain amount of nastiness from male professors, they hate to experience the same thing from a woman professor. At any rate, when I first started teaching and experimentally tried to use some of the milder verbal tactics I had heard from male 'maestri' – for example pouncing on them with the question, 'Why are you playing so boringly?' – I found that my students were hurt and surprised. Perhaps such tactics just didn't seem natural *coming from me*. I never knew whether it was to do with my personality or the fact that I was a woman. Not long ago, a friend who is a university teacher reported to me that her institution had done a survey of student attitudes towards their lecturers. The survey found that students tended to admire male lecturers who 'winged it' in their lectures, speaking without notes, but students disparaged female lecturers as 'under-prepared' and 'irresponsible' if they did the same thing. (My friend observed that 'speaking without notes' was a strange thing to admire because it probably meant that the lecturer concerned was leaving out a mass of fine detail impossible to memorise.) In group tutorials, students praised male teachers for being 'exciting', 'decisive' and 'objective', whereas they approved of female teachers who were 'caring' and 'empathetic'. Female tutors whose style resembled that of the male ones were often judged to be 'sharp', 'bossy' or 'unfriendly'. Female academics were much more likely to have their marking questioned by students. Male professors who shambled in to the lecture hall in the same moth-eaten jumpers and corduroy trousers they'd been wearing for twenty years were regarded as 'being at ease with themselves' whereas their casually-dressed female counterparts were 'not professional-looking'. The surveys were going to be published within the university and my friend commented that her students were going to get a big surprise when they saw how many gender stereotypes they were unconsciously carrying around with them.

When I think about the 'maestri' I've come across in masterclass situations, I realise that the overwhelming majority of them were male. If I run my inner eye over the 'tutor lists' of various courses and seminars I've been involved in, I find few female names. The same is true of international competition juries on which I've served. Is it just another example of the international 'old boys' network'? When you consider piano teaching for children – neighbourhood piano teachers or teachers working in schools – women are well represented in the profession, and perhaps they are even in the majority. But at the level of advanced performance teaching in public masterclasses, women professors are conspicuously in the minority. Why should that be? Are women being artificially kept out, or do they choose not to engage with these arenas? Are men suddenly entering the arena at the advanced level because public classes are the only kind of teaching they consider glamorous? In the wider field of concert pianism, women are still relatively few in number, so perhaps it is hardly surprising that they are in the minority in masterclass teaching situations too. But I suspect that there is something about the gladiatorial atmosphere which puts women off. It is a pity that masterclasses have acquired a reputation for 'theatre', because a combative environment is not a necessary ingredient of good teaching. Perhaps the dominance of male professors is analogous to the mysterious fact that most domestic cooks are women, whereas most famous chefs are men.

Different physiques

I remember once hearing a chamber music masterclass where, after a piano-and-violin duo had performed, a well-known Hungarian professor said dismissively to the two players, 'You only play it like that because you can't play it any other way.' The audience froze with horrified sympathy. He meant, presumably, that the musical 'interpretation' was simply the product of their limitations, not the result of artistic choice and decision.

Was it true that those students couldn't play it any other way? It struck me that 'technique' is the luxury of being able to play things in more than one way. When I consider the many things at which I'm not good – drawing, say, or chess or tennis – it's probably true that I only do them in the way I do them because I can't do them any other way. A result *of any kind* is all that's within my power. Technique is having a *choice* of how to do things. A musician who wants to be able to make many different tone colours must acquire the technique to do so. We all know the feeling of listening to a beginner or an amateur with a very limited technique and knowing that no more is to be expected of them because they are doing all that they can. They can't yet do it any other way. Everyone finds such a feeling acceptable when listening to a beginner – less so when listening to someone who's supposed to be at an advanced stage of attainment.

For all of us it is, of course, the case that we can only do what we can do. What we *want* has to be filtered through what we are *able* to do, and for most of us there is a gap between the two. Very few musicians can always play exactly as they wish to play. We can develop our powers but no matter how diligently we practise there will probably be some limits on, for example, how fast we can play and still remain accurate. When I listen to the recordings of, say, Vladimir Horowitz playing extremely fast with great precision, I recognise a nervous system with a higher gear than my own. It's a little like watching a champion runner like Usain Bolt: you just sense he has natural attributes which others don't possess and couldn't acquire through training. When I listen to Horowitz I don't feel that he simply practised more; I feel that he probably possessed neural pathways which processed information at speed better than most pianists' brains can. I don't set myself to practise for thousands of hours until I can play as fast as he did, because I sense that Nature has set some absolute limits on my physical co-ordination. When I listen to John Ogdon or Jorge Bolet thundering their way through Rachmaninov I don't feel that I could play with that kind of weight and amplitude if only I practised more: I sense that their sounds were linked to their physique. No doubt they *wanted* to play like that, but nature had also equipped them to do so.

Other musicians might *want* to play like that, but it doesn't come naturally to them. We often have to fight for a sound which contradicts our own physique. For a pianist with small hands, for example, there are many chords they won't be able to stretch such that all the notes go down at the same time. When chords stretch over more than an octave – a tenth is not unusual, and if there are several notes in the middle of the chord that makes it more strenuous – a pianist with small hands will have to 'roll' the chord, playing the notes in a rapid cascade from the bass upwards. This is usually perfectly fine, but it does mean that the dense, chunky sound of a big chord all of whose notes go down at the same time can never be part of their sound. (It's a curious thing that Chopin, whose hands were not large, often writes chords of more than an octave. Either he expected those chords to be rolled, or he was looking forward to hearing the music played by people with larger hands than his own.)

My own hands can comfortably stretch an octave and even a ninth if I have time to 'stretch for it', but not if it has to be played very quickly, or if there are several notes in between the top and bottom, forming a chord. I have never been able to produce the rich dense chords that a pianist with bigger hands can play. Rachmaninov was said to have been able to stretch a twelfth (an octave plus an interval of a fifth) on the piano, and he could play several notes in between as well, such as a chord of C-E-G-C-G). Such a stretch enabled him to produce a specific sonority, akin to a dark colour in painting. I hear the sound on recordings and recognise it as being one I've never heard myself make, except if I use two hands to play the chord. I don't feel too deprived, because there are some advantages to having small hands – agility, nimbleness, and so on. Indeed there are several pianists such as Alicia de Larrocha whose careers were not hampered by having small hands and who achieved amazing things by developing a lateral stretch.

The era of 1920s ragtime and syncopated piano music often has a characteristic boom-chink-boom-chink movement of the pianist's left hand, playing big bass chords on the main beats and jumping up an octave or two for lighter chords on the offbeats. When you hear one of the original composer-pianists doing this on a recording, it has a very characteristic sound as the full bass chords go down in blocks. I love that kind of music, but I can't put down those bass chords as written – I have to roll them. Rolling them means that they take up a fraction more time than they should, and the roll gives the music a slightly more Romantic-era feeling. To rewrite the chords so that they cover an octave instead of a tenth, eleventh or twelfth would remove important harmony notes. So I roll them, recognising that this has to be 'my way' of doing it because I am not Erroll Garner, able to span the huge chords with comfort.

Often one is called upon to play works which feel as if they were written for a different kind of player, or a player with a different physique. I, for example, always feel anxious when playing works like the Tchaikovsky Piano Trio, which calls for powerful muscular pianism. Yet if I love the piece and want to play it, I have to set out to meet its requirements, conscious that it may not seem to be an obvious fit between me and that particular piece. The effect is compounded when playing music of an era in which it would have been extremely rare, perhaps unheard of, to find a female pianist performing such a work in a public concert. If I want to perform the Tchaikovsky Trio, however, I have to rid myself of the idea that I will look ridiculous. In fact I have to work consciously at the idea that I look entirely comfortable. It certainly helps to have an image – derived from Russian literature – of myself as a strong and powerful storyteller, dispensing torrents of arpeggios as easily as adjectives. Without such an image, the task would feel beyond me. I say 'feel' rather than 'be' because with sufficient practice and a good imaginative concept, the task does actually move into my grasp. My mental image and my physical capacity start to align.

This, I think, is what the professor meant by saying that the students only played like that because they couldn't play any other way. He didn't feel they were playing what they *meant*, but rather what they *could*. He despised them because their musical desires were not stronger. But one might also say that as a teacher he failed to be able to stimulate their imaginations. Indeed, in the long run his remark was probably a guarantee that their imaginations would be forever stifled when they returned to that particular piece of music, because their memories of it would be tinged with pain.

Most people who get to masterclass level have developed their imagination along with their love of music. An appeal to the imagination can help a student to go beyond their apparent physical limitations and enable them to surprise people with a sonority they weren't expecting. Sándor Végh used to say that the biggest tone he ever heard from a violin was made by the French violinist Ginette Neveu – 'a small girl!' Ginette Neveu (1919–49) may have been small, but clearly she possessed the *will* to sound big, which is half the battle. Her understanding of the principles of balance and weight when applying bow to string (you can see it in photographs of her playing) allowed her to produce a far bigger tone than she 'should' have been capable of. Likewise the Argentinian pianist Martha Argerich, not a large or powerful person to look at, has amazed audiences throughout her career with her strength and speed as well as her determination to achieve the result she wants, which appears to be possible for her even after periods of time in which she plays very few public concerts. In these and similar cases, 'mind over matter' is the only way to describe the principle at work. It seems to boil down to the ability to envisage a sound and a result so strongly that one's physical powers are put at the service of the imagination and not – as is the case for many people – the other way round.

The inescapability of
one's own nature

Just as musicians have to work with their innate physical capabilities, when it comes to matters of interpretation they cannot help being guided at least to some extent by their own temperament and emotional nature. Here again, imagination can act as a powerful escape route. Even if someone is an introvert and has a natural tendency to feel music as sad, inward or thoughtful, a dose of imagination can liberate them. An extrovert whose natural impulse is to 'show off' the music in its most sparkling or colourful aspect can use their imagination to find elements of shadow or regret. Good musicians have to learn to be like barristers in court, capable of presenting either side of the argument if required to do so. It is certainly true that a good musician can make a very convincing case for music which goes against their individual nature. But there is something emotionally tiring about presenting a musical case which doesn't come naturally to you. I suppose this is why most performers gravitate towards repertoire for which nature and intellect have best equipped them.

A good musician will work towards creating a bond between the composer's mind and their own, so that when they play the music it seems as if it is emanating from them. It's often said that 'interpreters' are not creative artists, but I think most serious interpreters would say that their work does indeed feel creative. They know that before it reaches other people, music must be embodied in sound and that they are its embodiment. The composer has necessarily stepped back and the player has stepped forward to make the music happen. If they succeed in creating a bond between their mind and the composer's, they will create a dynamic of performance. We've all been to concerts where there is no bond between the player and the music, where nothing more compelling than 'playing the notes' seems to underlie the performance. When I go to concerts I dread having to witness an empty space between the player and the music.

How to fill that empty space? It's important to have filled it by using your imagination long before you arrive on stage. Sometimes in a concert one senses that the 'empty space' is being filled there and then by showing off. But most serious musicians do the work ahead of time. If you are an introvert and the music strikes you as thoughtful and confiding, it is helpful to explore that thought because as you do so, your listeners will recognise an alchemical bond between the music and you. If you are an extrovert and you feel that the music is bursting to be expressed in glorious virtuoso flourishes, then your audience will feel comfortable with your approach. Is this another way of saying that 'you only play that way because you can't play any other way'? Perhaps there is a sense in which this observation is indeed profoundly true, and it can be a compliment as well as an insult. Audiences will recognise that you 'cannot tell a lie'.

Art has many twists and turns, however, and it can sometimes be helpful for a player and an image they have cultivated to be prised apart. Once or twice during György Sebők's piano masterclasses I saw him pull a trick on a student who was tensing up before a particularly difficult passage in the music. Sebők used to sit at a second piano next to the student pianist and once, as a student was labouring towards the most difficult bit, I saw him catch her eye with a smile and point to a spot in the corner by the ceiling, as though something delicious were to be seen there. Without ceasing to play, the student followed his pointing finger and looked upwards. Simultaneously, to our amazement, we heard her play the difficult passage effortlessly. Realising that she had just played it without her usual furious concentration, she stopped and said, 'Oh! What just happened?'

Sebök explained that by distracting her he had interfered with her usual pattern: over-concentrating as she approached the dreaded passage. He wanted to demonstrate to her that she *had* practised the notes and *could* play them, if only she could stop self-doubt creeping in and telling her otherwise. Her feelings of inadequacy had become ingrained in her method of tackling this difficult passage, and her tension was working against her physical freedom. But when he flicked her attention elsewhere by pointing to something in the room at a crucial moment, she was sidetracked – and her hands took over. It turned out that her muscle memory was equal to the task. Obviously this doesn't work if you haven't done the practice, but she *had* done it. It proved to all of us that, if she could stop anticipating failure, she was capable of playing it perfectly well. Sebök's trick, applied with forensic timing, seemed almost like witchcraft, but we all realised its psychological accuracy.

Having been the 'victim', or one might rather say the fortunate recipient of such a trick, how can you repeat the effect when there is no teacher there to play a trick on you, and you are once more alone in your practice studio? Some students can profit more than others from such an experience. For some, the experience of having a metaphorical blade slipped between their technique and their tangle of thoughts about it can be profoundly liberating. For others, the experience will remain a tantalising glimpse of paradise.

What we talk about in lessons

When the members of my Piano Club talk about their early music lessons, they often comment that important musical topics were not addressed. Perhaps they have forgotten what their teachers really said (we all tend to), but when they think back to those days they claim that the emphasis was on accuracy, 'playing nicely', notching up their daily practice, passing the next grade exam and making their parents and teachers proud. Indeed it is the alleged 'boringness' of early piano lessons that leads many to give them up when they are allowed to. Many students, from different parts of the world, have told me similar stories. I often feel sad – sometimes even enraged – to think how much their relationship with music has been complicated by unsympathetic lessons in childhood.

Learning a musical instrument is many children's first experience of a pastime which requires them to develop discipline (or at least requires them to heed a parent summoning them to do their music practice). The challenges of grade exams and 'competition festivals', designed to provide milestones of achievement, are welcomed by some children but feared and resented by others. Learning music can slip from being a pastime to becoming a chore, sometimes even a penance, and naturally this reflects on children's attitudes to the teachers. It also makes teachers feel that, like it or not, they have to be taskmasters. New and 'fun' approaches to music education are always being devised, but nothing can take away from the fact that young learners have to apply themselves day after day and week after week if they want to learn an instrument properly. Many who begin by thinking that it would be jolly to be able to play some music end up feeling that the downside is too great. Even I, a child who basically enjoyed it, often found myself thinking 'I don't want to do it *this* much.' In a way it would be good if music education could be left for later years, but the plasticity of the brain is greatest in youth, and learning when you are young is an opportunity not to be missed.

I feel I was fortunate because all my teachers sincerely liked music, liked teaching and guiding me through some of the classics of piano repertoire. I looked forward to my lessons and never felt I was treading water. But judging from the number of discouraging anecdotes I've heard and the number of people who've told me that they struggled to hold on to their sense of joy in playing, much early learning is humdrum. When I draw people's attention to the shifting moods of a piece of music they learned in childhood, or ask them what the moods relate to in their own lives, they often comment with a certain wistfulness that their teachers never discussed such matters with them and they wish they had had more practice at considering them. I suppose it comes back to the same old problem that playing the piano is a complex physical task, and there is plenty to work on without getting seduced by open questions of musical meaning. My first lesson notebooks, in which music teachers wrote my 'homework tasks', were filled with almost exclusively practical advice and I imagine it is the same for most young musicians. Nevertheless we must never lose sight of the fact that we play music because it is evocative, and because it creates a haven for the mind. If there is anything which will keep young musicians focused on the task of mastering an instrument, it is this. Perhaps the spiritual side of music is too often left for the individual to discover privately, when it could be woven into discussions along the way.

'How to practise' is another topic which (allegedly) was rarely addressed. The subject could fill a book of its own. For now, suffice it to say that advice on practising often seems to have been confined to 'play it over and over again'. This is necessary advice, but repeating things for hours on end is not the only way to make progress. Practising in your head is equally important and sometimes more effective when it comes to imagining musical shape and atmosphere, because you're not preoccupied by the mechanics of playing. Learning to 'hear' music in your imagination is a crucial part of becoming a better musician. Liszt said, 'Think ten times and play once'.

My adult students also say that nobody ever spoke to them about how or in what way our musical approach should change when we play in public. What should we focus on when we play to other people? Are we showing off or sharing? Should our attitude be one of confidence or humility? You might think that this is the subject of deep discussion between teacher and pupil, but many students have told me that the only performance advice they were given was to make sure to 'play out', 'project', and 'think of playing to the person in the back row'! Of course such advice is well meant, but I've realised that it is not helpful. If you fixate on playing to the people in the back row, you are likely to lose touch with your own moment-by-moment musical thoughts. To give blanket advice to 'play out' is like telling a cook that when they prepare an array of dishes for paying diners they should smother everything in hot sauce at the last moment, no matter how delicate the ingredients or how artfully contrasted.

Many novice performers seem to think (and indeed go on thinking for years) that when they find themselves in the spotlight, they should start declaiming, even if they never did so at home. If you remind them that when *they* are in the audience they don't like to be 'shouted at', they readily agree. But once on the platform, they can become fixated on a rigid notion of projecting to the back row. Sadly, this can separate them from their normal musical and thinking selves. Being a performer is already a big enough change of mental state without also feeling mysteriously obliged to play in a different way. Attempting to 'play out' all the time makes everything feel technically different and more effortful. As well as being tiring, it is disorienting and can make the player feel foreign to themselves, often producing the dreaded sensation of 'not being properly there' – an experience which makes people wary of performing in public again. Instead of merely being told to project, students should be encouraged to consider what they want the audience to realise about the music and to think about how that is to be communicated. This is not to say that the people in the back row should be shut out of the performer's mental picture, but they should be included rather than bombarded. If the audience senses that the musician has something to say, they will try to hear it, even when they are sitting in the back row. It's much better to draw the audience in, make them lean forward to catch subtle nuances or to empathise with the performer's own quiet absorption. I have tried both approaches – 'playing out' and 'drawing in' – and feel much more at home with the latter. I don't like to think of the stress suffered by players who feel they must scale everything up for public performance.

Parkinson's Law states that 'work expands to fill the time available', and I think this applies to weekly piano lessons. Young minds could be more engaged, things could be made more interesting, and the technique of playing an instrument could probably be more quickly learned – as is also the case with many subjects we are taught at school. But on the other side of the equation are the systems of learning we have set up, the structure of exams, and the economic realities of life for teachers and schools, not to mention the realities of life for working parents who are glad to think of their children being safely occupied in educational pursuits. For sure, some aspects of musical expertise benefit from being slowly and methodically learned over dozens of individual lessons. Other aspects could be taught more imaginatively and learned more quickly, but then how would the lessons be filled? One can see that it makes sense to parcel out the learning process in an extended series of lessons, but unfortunately it also seems to lead to many teachers (and therefore pupils) losing their enthusiasm for the subject.

Of course it's also true that a teacher can say exactly the right thing, but there is no meaningful 'knowledge transfer' if the student is not ready to hear it. I'm sure my teachers said many wise things which passed me by at the time. If I could meet them again and tell them of the important insights I devoured at a later stage, they might well tear their hair and say, 'But I told you that when you were a child!' As a teacher one always hopes that when one thinks of a really helpful thing to say, one's student will be in the perfect mood to hear it and act on it. But it's not easy to achieve that perfect collaboration, because many students feel defensive at their lessons, and many (especially those who are studying piano at someone else's behest) spend their lesson time preoccupied with other things entirely. As a teacher I know all too well that feeling of having given a helpful bit of advice which the student hasn't really 'heard'. Very occasionally a student will contact me later to say that they have suddenly understood what I was talking about, but such moments are rare and cherished. I have also been surprised to learn which of my comments were helpful. For example, I gave a consultation lesson to one young professional pianist during which I felt I had 'nailed' all kinds of things, especially about her approach to musical shaping. We worked and worked on making the shape clear and exploring what it revealed about the inner emotion. I was happy to think of her going home with new ways of working. About six months afterwards she wrote to thank me for mentioning in passing that she was sitting with the piano stool too low. Changing the height of the stool had altered her posture, and her back no longer ached when she practised. She didn't mention anything else. These moments are their own lessons in perspective.

At any rate, whether or not the members of my Piano Club were told important things about music when they were young learners, I find they are ready to hear things now. In fact they are much less focused on hearing technical tips and tricks than they are on encountering 'big' musical ideas. We often find that 'big' ideas lead to small things being resolved. For example, just drawing someone's attention to the melodic line threaded through a long phrase, and asking them to make us understand that line, will help them to 'ignore' or experience in a different perspective the difficulties of fast-moving inner parts instead of obsessing over them. And people often respond very well to being asked to imagine a piece of music like a journey through a landscape. When are they walking, when are they resting, when are they at the top of a hill? When is it rough terrain, when can they coast easily downhill? When can they see a long way ahead? When is the landscape cast into shadow? If they can conceive of the music in those terms, can they make us understand those elements of the journey?

It's interesting to watch how students of all kinds respond to realising that a 'concept' can accelerate their progress. One might think that anyone would be overjoyed to find out that something is easy, but it isn't as simple as that. Finding that things are easy runs counter to all sorts of cultural beliefs and work ethics, themselves the props of a person's self-esteem and the milestones which help them to structure their time. How will they structure their time if things turn out to be easy? Will it mean that their work has been for nothing, or that they have been working at the wrong thing? Will it mean that the need for a long training has been mis-sold to them? For some, a glimpse of the shortcut to the top will seem like sleight of hand. *Does it mean anything without suffering?* Finding themselves suddenly at the top, they will feel that something important has been denied them, as if a helicopter had whisked them through the sky and deposited them at the summit when they had dedicated their life to the idea of climbing the mountain step by arduous step. For some, the experience of 'ease' will trigger a whole new set of questions leading to thousands of more hours in the practice studio. For others, being shown that something is easy will allow them to *stop* asking questions. It gives you a profound sense of satisfaction to climb a mountain step by step, and you feel proud of yourself.

But no matter how you get to the summit, the view from the top is exactly the same.

When I started my Piano Club, I was inspired by having heard about Eliane Lust's 'studio' for non-professional pianists in San Francisco. Eliane told me that the moment she realised her studio was a success was when its members started meeting without her, attending one another's concerts and organising Pot Luck suppers. The same has happened to me. My Piano Club has developed its own social life, and has proved to me that pianists can generously support one another. People go to each other's performances, lend each other interesting music, arrange to play piano duets, meet up for dinner before going to a concert (perhaps one of mine). It gives me great satisfaction to think of this little group of pianists who have become friends. And although my Piano Club started off as a kind of outreach project, they have reached out to me as well.

The benefit of hindsight

Elisa (not her real name) was a lovely pianist who, like me, was very keen on chamber music. She occasionally came for a lesson on solo repertoire. I never had to tell her to think about the music, because I knew she would do that anyway.

She played the opening of Schubert's last piano sonata very slowly and gravely, bending over the keys as if bowed down by the cares of the world.

'Why are you playing it so slowly?' I wondered. 'It's marked "molto moderato". That's not a slow marking.'

'I'm playing it slowly because I know how sadly it turns out in the end', she said. 'I've been thinking about it for ages. I can't un-know what I know about it, can I?'

This is the performer's conundrum. When we play a piece for others to hear, how do we bring it freshly to life for someone hearing it for the first time? We have to know and yet not know.

In this Schubert sonata, the opening is a simple, restrained melody marked to be played quietly and at a moderate pace. Apart from the mysterious trill in the bass, there are no intimations of anything darker. As we get to know the whole piece, we discover that the opening melody was only the first step in a journey which moves through some long and unexpected diversions to a sadder place. By the time we get to the end, we are in a position to look back and shake our heads wonderingly at the first steps and how simple they seemed.

Does this mean that, next time we play it, we should make it clear from the first bars that we know what is waiting round the corner? Or is it our task to present the music as simply as the composer presents it to us?

'Suppose there are people in the audience who've never heard this piece before', I said. 'If you start like that, very slowly and sadly, you're denying them a chance to experience how Schubert covers a lot of emotional ground between the beginning and the end. Schubert starts simply and so should you.'

'But I don't hear the beginning as "simple" any more', Elisa objected. 'If I played it like that, I'd be pretending. I'm the one who's playing the piece. Shouldn't my performance be coloured by my understanding of it?'

'I don't want you to pretend', I said. 'You know the piece, so you have the benefit of hindsight. You can use that to put things in the right perspective for the audience. If you play the opening very slowly and sadly, you want them to be impressed by *your* understanding of the piece. Of course it's important that you understand it, but when you perform it, the focus should switch to them. They need to know that everything feels quiet and serene at the start. And then they need to "get" the big changes as they happen. If you can make them see those, they will understand the piece as Schubert meant them to.'

'So maybe it's like when I'm reading a child a story', she said. 'I wouldn't put on a sad voice when Sleeping Beauty first appears, just because I know she's going to prick her finger and fall asleep for a hundred years. I'd make her seem like a happy young girl.'

'Yes, you would,' I agreed, 'partly because you wouldn't have practised and practised reading this story aloud in an empty room for months before you actually read it to a real live child. If you had a child to read to, you'd instinctively try not to spoil the story by letting them in on the secret of what happens. You might even start reading without remembering how the story ends!'

We both sighed.

'Things get so complicated for us pianists', I said. 'We spend so long on these pieces. We become more and more aware of what *we* understand. But we must try not to be self-centred. What does the listener need to understand?'

Fusion cooking

Music-making, like everything else, has been subjected to processes of globalisation over recent decades, and classical musicians of the highest order now come from all around the world. One of the greatest successes at the Proms in recent years was the Simón Bolívar Youth Orchestra under their charismatic young conductor, Gustavo Dudamel, all of them trained in Venezuela's groundbreaking 'Sistema' programme of musical education.

It's been particularly striking how many excellent musicians now come from East Asia, and I have encountered many of them in my playing, teaching and work on competition juries. Classical music has been so thoroughly absorbed by musicians from across the globe now that there is little sense that this music 'belongs' to Europeans in the way that we used to assume that it did, and the old stereotypes about how people from different cultures might approach this music are, one hopes, long gone. Nevertheless I have found in my teaching experience that other cultures have preserved some of their traditional ways of teaching, different from what we are used to in Europe, and I find it a fascinating experience to be in dialogue with these diverse traditions.

I have a Japanese friend in Tokyo who every spring sends me

many photographs of cherry trees and other blossoms to be viewed in the Imperial Gardens, the Botanical Gardens and other parks round about the capital. The photos are carefully captioned with the names of each type of tree and of blossom. I have read a little about the Japanese love of cherry trees and the tradition of making pilgrimages to admire their flowers in spring, but I don't know enough about it to get a deep sense of what it really means to the Japanese connoisseur. I enjoy the photos partly because I sense from the careful labelling that there is deep meaning and pleasure for the connoisseur in this experience.

I find myself looking forward to the cherry blossom photos because through his attention to detail my Japanese friend has managed to communicate that he wants *me* to get meaning from the experience. This is something I want to live up to. Even if I cannot match his level of appreciation, I enjoy second-hand his deep appreciation of the pale pinks, whites, deep pinks, white tinged with pale pink, pink with a hint of lilac, pink shading to peach, drooping branches, heavily laden branches, and the delicate perfume of the different types of cherry blossom trees.

When I pore over the photos, training myself to note the differences, does that mean I have acquired the Japanese culture of 'hanami', the appreciation of cherry blossom? I know that the blossom is valued precisely because of its transience. That's an approach I instinctively share. The cherry trees flower so beautifully but so briefly, prompting thoughts of brief lives. For a very long time the Japanese have cultivated 'mujo', the sense that nothing is permanent, that everything changes and comes to an end. This is not something sad, but something we must learn to accept in a positive spirit. Rejoicing as the cherry blossoms appear, appreciating them no less as the petals fade and fall to the ground, is a demonstration of how to submit to impermanence. In a sense, therefore, to capture these blossoms in photos, to catalogue them and keep them on your computer, runs contrary to the spirit of cherry blossom appreciation. When I look at the photos I wonder how I, a foreigner, can ever penetrate this ancient culture. Without knowing the history, the religion, the literature and poetry, I am only a well-meaning observer. Yet I don't come empty-handed to this experience. Perhaps there is a sense in which I, with my western sensibility, might even be able to bring something new to this exchange. I don't understand the cherry blossoms as a cultured Japanese person would, but I do have frames of reference and a background in poetry and literature which allows me to understand them in my own way. Maybe there are even things I could reflect back to my Japanese friend which might prompt some new thoughts in him about his beloved cherry blossoms?

After giving a recital at an American university a few years ago, I was invited to give a lecture about my experience of being a classical musician. What changes had I observed in the course of my professional life? In the talk I happened to speak about the rapidly growing trend for students to come from China, Korea and Japan to study western classical music at European conservatories. Western music has been popular in those countries for a long time – in Japan, the Tokyo Philharmonic was founded in 1911 and the NHK Symphony Orchestra in 1926, while in South Korea, symphony orchestras were established in the 1950s. China's long dialogue with western classical music was catastrophically interrupted during the Cultural Revolution of 1966–76, but in the decades since then they have been returning with appetite to this previously forbidden music.

Nevertheless when I was a student myself, as far as I recall I had not a single fellow student from East Asia. A few years later, when attending international music courses in the 1980s, I started to meet students from Japan. Some years after that I started to meet Korean students, but still none from China. But when the internal situation in China became more favourable to foreign study, there was suddenly a flood of students from China. When I began to do some masterclass teaching, some of my first students were from China and Korea, and I was thrilled to meet them. Many of them were outstanding players whose level of preparation and work ethic put them way ahead of most of their European counterparts. They recognised how lucky we were to have a vast written repertoire and were eager to learn about the cultural attitudes and the artistic principles which made European artists play the way they did. Indeed the best of them were desperate not to be identifiable as 'foreigners' when they played Beethoven and Brahms. They soaked up any information I could give them about idiomatic ways to play this repertoire.

Today there are so many Chinese students at UK conservatoires and universities that when walking down the corridors of those buildings one sometimes has the impression of being in Shanghai or Beijing rather than Manchester or Glasgow. When I am invited to do some guest teaching at a music conservatory, or to adjudicate a competition, I now expect that half of the students will be from East Asia. Delightful as these students often are, the sight of so many of them in a European conservatory makes me feel as if I'm witnessing an important transition in the history of classical music, but one that I don't quite understand. What does it mean that our home-grown students are ambivalent about studying at our conservatories, while so many East Asian students are queuing up to do so? As far as I know there is no counterpart in British students clamouring to study Chinese or Korean music in Shanghai, Beijing or Seoul.

A colleague of mine who recently played in China told me that so many young people wanted to attend his concerts that the organisers had to put a limit on the number of tickets available to young people, in order to give other age groups a chance. In all my years of concert-giving in the west I have never encountered such a situation and can scarcely even imagine the thrill of having crowds of young people desperate to attend my concerts. I felt stirred and deeply envious. At the same time, this is such a tsunami of enthusiasm that one has to wonder whether it is a true cultural shift or merely a passing fashion.

As yet, nobody knows how long the 'fashion moment' will persist or whether it will mature into a long-lasting relationship. Coming from such a different culture, can these young musicians really understand European art music, or are they as dazed as I am when I contemplate hundreds of almost identical cherry blossom photos? Does it matter if they don't understand our music in the way that we do, as long as they love it? Could it be that they appreciate it more than we do? There is no doubt that for many of these young musicians, their connection to western classical music is intense and heartfelt. Might they be well suited to become its guardians? After all, when we read history we discover that various kinds of learning have passed from one culture into the stewardship of another. It seems that the society which originated the discoveries can also lose track of them and even cease to value them, while other cultures may see the point of them and welcome the opportunity to build on them, sometimes passing them back in better condition to a culture which had forgotten about them.

Personally, I welcome the appearance of East Asian musicians on the scene because since teenage years I have been fascinated by the culture of what we used to call 'the Far East'. In fact I often think that if I could choose which part of the world to come from, I might choose that part. Oriental art, literature and in particular Zen Buddhism have been amongst my profoundest influences, as readers of my previous books will have realised. I was that starstruck teenager with a copy of Lao Tzu and poems by Li Po and Tu Fu (as we called Li Bai and Du Fu then) on my bedside table. Since student years I've always had posters and prints of Chinese and Japanese art on the walls of wherever I was living. I love the aesthetic which values the jewel-like haiku, the Zen rock garden, the calligraphy that derives its character from what is being written, the handmade bowl which expresses the ingredients of the moment when it was thrown. I may be missing specific cultural references and resonances, but my own life experience enables me to vibrate in sympathy with the spiritual qualities of oriental art. I particularly like the attitude which prizes restraint as something positive and meaningful rather than something empty or negative, as it can be seen in the west. When

I first started to meet students from Japan, China and Korea I felt that in some ways I was already on their wavelength, and even that we had many things in common, including our sense of humour. Clearly this is to some extent an illusion, because my knowledge of Asian culture is superficial, but nevertheless it is very appealing to me, and I have always felt very comfortable working with students from that part of the world.

Today, Asian students spend enormous sums of money on coming to the USA and Europe to take their music diplomas and degrees. Because most of the classical repertoire is from Europe, they particularly prize a European diploma. They tell me that being the student of a well-known European classical performer is a feather in their cap when they go home again. It is curious to witness all this while at the same time in the UK there is a feeling, running in completely the opposite direction, that studying classical music is old-fashioned or 'elitist' and that all today's really relevant musicians are in pop music. The same classical music professor whose name adds lustre to a Chinese student's CV is probably unknown to his or her neighbours in the British street where he or she lives, at least in terms of their professional achievements.

When I was talking about all this in my American lecture, I said that it was strange to observe this clash of attitudes. In my own country, there is widespread disengagement from classical music, while at the same time our music colleges are overflowing with bright, eager, fashion-conscious students from East Asia energised by their quest to become successful classical musicians. A friend of mine teaches at a music conservatoire in Germany where, every time they hold auditions for places in the next year's string classes, coachloads of Korean students turn up and outshine most of the local candidates with their impressive technical skills and their clear sense of goals. It was strange, he said, to see the coaches drive up to the ornate nineteenth-century portals and the Korean students pile out with their instruments. But: 'How can one not like teaching them? They are so hard-working and motivated.'

Indeed they are, and I shall always remember the satisfaction of working with the brilliant young Korean violinist, Sulki Yu. I was organising another round of my London masterclasses in piano and string chamber music, and in 2010 I decided to make the bold experiment of reversing the usual roles of student and 'accompanist'. Normally in such classes the focus is the string player, and a pianist is tasked with playing the piano parts of any and all pieces the string players bring to the class. Sometimes the pianist will know the works concerned, sometimes not, but in either event they are expected to be able to give a plausible rendering of whatever it is without having a nervous breakdown when the volume of music is put in front of them. This one-pianist-for-everyone arrangement is practical, but often has the regrettable side-effect of making the piano parts seem less important than they should be. It struck me that it might be eye-opening for all concerned to turn the formula around, make the pianists the focus and ask one single violinist if he or she would be willing to stand there for the whole weekend and play the violin part of any duo sonata that a pianist wanted to work on. I had never seen it done this way round, but why not? Pianists are routinely asked to play anything from a huge repertoire, and nobody seems to think the task is superhuman.

But when I started explaining my idea to string players and asking if they'd like to star in my experiment, there was a sharp intake of breath and a shocked or 'amused' refusal: far too demanding, they said, too risky, unrealistic, much too tiring, couldn't possibly do it without working out the fingering ahead of time, might look foolish, and so on. I began to think I'd have to give up my role-reversal idea. As the time drew near, I asked advice from the highly-regarded violin professor David Takeno, who instantly said, 'Sulki Yu. She is the one you want!' I didn't know her, but I got in touch, explained the concept of the classes, and she agreed to do it. She didn't say any of the things about it being too risky or demanding. And when it came to the classes, I saw in action the combination of intelligence, quickness, technical prowess, calm, poise and determination which seems to characterise the best East Asian musicians. Sulki stood there in front of our listeners and quietly faced up to every challenge given her by the pianists over two long days, including a final concert with several different pianists. In each session she listened to my advice and took it on board, just as if the lesson was for her. At one point we were working on the first movement of the violin and piano sonata by César Franck. I tried to outline the 'big picture' over the whole of the opening section, indicating the ideal shape that would knit everything together in a big arc. Sulki listened carefully and then, without even having the opportunity to try anything out in private, she played it again with such a perfect and instant realisation of the shape I had sketched out that I had tears in my eyes, and I wasn't the only one.

After my talk at the American university, there was a question-and-answer session. A historian stood up and commented that 'culture has always been migratory'. What I had described, he said, was just the evidence that interest in classical music was declining in the west, but was becoming more and more valued in the east. We used to think of Germany and Austria as being the heartland of classical music, but today it looks more and more as if China and Korea are the places where it is regarded as a high-status educational goal and a worthy career aspiration. Did it matter, he asked, who were the custodians of classical music as long as *someone* was? We should just relax and look at classical music as a ball which was being slowly bounced around the world. Maybe pianists in Europe are putting up with unsatisfactory, under-maintained pianos in many concert venues, but in China the conservatories are shipping in dozens of brand-new Steinway grands. Because the Chinese market is so important, Chinese rules on which woods and materials may be imported are already leading to changes in the way that major western piano manufacturers make new pianos. While we in the west are exchanging the old pianos in our apartments for digital keyboards (so much less annoying for the neighbours), millions of Chinese children, many of them inspired by the superstar pianist

Lang Lang, are learning the piano and aspiring to have proper 'old-fashioned' pianos in their homes.

Perhaps one should look on tranquilly as classical music 'migrates' to other parts of the world, but I find that while *sharing* it feels like a splendid idea, I don't want to wave goodbye to it for good as it sails off to a new life on distant shores. I worry about how much of its flavour and meaning will survive the journey. I'm glad that students in East Asia want to immerse themselves in western classical music, but I really hope they will want to understand its cultural context. The music which originated in Germany and Austria (or any European country) speaks to some extent in the language of that country and is perhaps even influenced by that country's air and weather. It is shaped by the cultural context it was made in, and by the instruments that were available. Its performance traditions are closely linked to the way society worked at any given period. Its range and types of expression are expressive of the attitudes of its time. The public's taste, musicians' expectations, the settings in which music was performed, the types of dances that were popular ... all these have to be understood if the music is to keep its dimensionality. The pieces of music themselves may have appeal across the world, but they are not divorced from the ground in which they grew. Mozart, for example, is internationally beloved, but to get the true flavour of his music one should know something about the sound of his piano, the rooms in which his music was played, the type of audiences who attended his concerts, the art and literature of his time, the politics and social realities which influenced his attitudes and his view of the world. Knowing something about his sense of humour and love of wordplay is a help. Ideally, one would know something about the kind of music which his grew out of, what he influenced, and in what way his music was and continues to be unique. His music has absolute value, I believe, but there is a danger in just plucking it out of its context and studying the notes of his music without having a sense of how it would have resonated with those who first heard it, and why. It gives me immense satisfaction to think of millions of East Asian children learning Mozart piano sonatas and concertos, but I fear for what may be lost if 'just the notes' are transplanted without a flavour of their cultural and historical setting. Of course, the finest artists will always be alert to this background, but when so many musicians of all levels are taking up western classical music, not everyone will be so attentive.

On the other hand I recognise that, quite apart from anxieties about 'preservation', students from other cultures can add something new to an existing culture and even re-invigorate it. Their sensibility may lead them to give priority to elements we've neglected. I already see that Chinese and Korean students have brought rigour and discipline to the task of becoming western-style musicians. They don't float about in an unfocused realm of 'art for art's sake', but rather view western music as an actual career which can bring them high status if they are successful. They work hard and plan their next steps. When London music colleges first started opening their practice rooms early in the morning, I was told that the people most eager to book the rooms were students from East Asia. Some of their European fellow students, who favoured 'inspiration' over planning, were a tiny bit dismissive of such zeal until they saw the results in the form of prizes and concert opportunities. Now everyone wants to practise early in the morning, and the standard of playing is rising all the time. I would say that the arrival of East Asian musicians has been energising for everyone.

The interactions between different cultures and traditions are, of course, complex and subtle. For every instance of a foreign tradition being joyfully welcomed into a new country, there seems to be one where the guardians of a tradition fear its dilution or even its loss. 'Fusion cooking', for example, blending western and oriental techniques and ingredients to produce surprising and delightful hybrids, is very popular, but for every fan of fusion cooking there is a connoisseur determined to protect the precious traditions of, say, Italian cookery where ways of making certain dishes have been passed down from generation to generation and valued all the more because they have remained authentic and unchanged. For guardians of this tradition, it is not amusing when a famous restaurant on the other side of the world updates a simple classic sauce with chilli, garlic or Pacific Rim seafood to make it 'contemporary'. I was struck recently when a British newspaper asked some Japanese sushi chefs for their views on mass-produced sushi available from UK supermarkets. All the chefs said that it was not sushi as they knew it, and that the fish was not 'fresh' as they would define it, so it was really a different dish. Mass-produced sushi has become very popular in the UK, and when we buy it we happily believe we are eating Japanese food, even though it's often a pale imitation of the Japanese classic.

In a competition like BBC Young Dancer, one can see a fascinating mix of cultures: there are categories which focus on one particular style, such as classical ballet or South Asian dance, but also categories which allow the performer to combine whatever elements take their fancy from different traditions and call it 'contemporary' or 'free' dance. In these open categories, one can see ballet elements being blended with street dance, and often the result is an extension of the expressive possibilities. But crossover categories also make many people uneasy; they fear that if the old boundaries are allowed to be erased, important elements of their own culture will fade away. Being open to new things is all very well, but living in constant flux is disorienting. Globalisation brings up this anxiety at every level, from trivial concerns about fusion cooking to worries about identity being lost. We are confronted every day with new influences arriving and with old influences waning. Who can say what new and valuable traditions will be created, or which old traditions will vanish? Will we be stronger or weaker when our traditions are taken up elsewhere? Many people in Europe find it surprising that so many oriental musicians want to study western art music, but they do, and their influence will change it, as well as our way of hearing it.

'You'll find the black notes play louder than the white ones'

On the 1966 comedy LP *Once Moore with Cook*, Peter Cook and Dudley Moore have a wonderful sketch in which Mr Stigwell, a rich and pompous businessman, comes for a piano lesson with a struggling Welsh piano teacher living in a cramped flat in Upminster and charging seven shillings and sixpence per half-hour. The businessman explains that he has no musical training and has never played the piano, but is in a hurry to learn to play Beethoven's Fifth Symphony by Tuesday week as a birthday treat for his wife. He declares, 'I know the basics of the piano: there are black notes and white notes, and the black notes play louder than the white ones.'

'No, sir, someone's been leading you up the garden path', the teacher (played by Dudley Moore) corrects him. He tries to explain how the piano really works, but his pupil is too impatient to listen. Eventually Mr Stigwell offers to pay the teacher many times more than his usual fee if he can just hurry up and teach him how to play Beethoven's Fifth. In anguished tones the teacher expostulates, 'Mr Stigwell, let me tell you that however rich you are, I can't accelerate the process of musical tuition! You can't buy musical talent like a pound of sausages!' He explains it is an impossible task for several reasons, not least the fact that Beethoven's Fifth Symphony is an orchestral piece. Integrity, he declares, is more important than money and he is not willing to lie to a pupil for money. 'I can't be bought! I'm not some sort of a musical harlot!' There's a dramatic pause and then Mr Stigwell says admiringly, 'First class. Nobody has spoken to me like that for years. Integrity! That's a valuable thing, and I'm willing to pay for it.' He offers Mr Stigwell a hundred guineas an hour to teach him Beethoven's Fifth by Tuesday week. At this mouthwatering prospect, the teacher caves in and agrees to do it. The lesson ends with him saying to the pupil, 'And I think you'll find that the black notes play a little louder than the white ones.'

I knew this sketch off by heart and could quote the whole thing when I was a teenager. It opened my eyes to the possibility of a link between the amount that a teacher was paid and the information they would be minded to dispense. I sometimes wondered what I could get my piano teachers to say and how helpful they would be about my future career if they were paid vast amounts – or indeed, what they might say if they weren't being paid as much as they were. Could they be bothered to say anything to me if they weren't being paid at all? Or might it even be that they would be *more* honest if money wasn't involved? Happily I can report from my own experience both of teaching and being taught, most music teachers give it their best shot regardless of how much money is being paid. It's not a totally straightforward situation, naturally, because when any skill becomes 'monetised', fine calibrations enter the equation, just as they do when – for example – you opt to be treated privately for a health problem. Though I have no doubt that doctors do their best no matter what the financial context, we've all heard that if you are paying privately, your doctor is likely to have more time for you, will organise your operation to suit your schedule, and will come and visit you afterwards to chat to you and check on your progress as you recover. Piano lessons are not really to be compared with medical appointments, but in a similar way I admit that when, for example, someone has travelled a long distance to come for a lesson – maybe flying in from another country – I resolve that I must rack my brains to say something truly useful to them while they're here, otherwise it will be a waste of their money. I feel as though they have invested in my company, so to speak, and I have a responsibility to them. This is not to say that my ears are less open when I give someone some free advice, but it cannot be denied that there is some kind of subtle relationship between money and the perceived pressure to provide value. Wanting to give a great lesson for a professional fee seems to me, however, a benign example of the relationship between money and advice; I can't imagine that any 'Mr Stigwell' could bribe me to say that the black notes play louder than the white ones.

When I was a student, I had a violinist friend who revered the great Russian violinist Nathan Milstein, and was ecstatic when he discovered that Milstein was living in London. Milstein was by temperament a performer rather than a teacher, but my friend persuaded Milstein to give him occasional lessons, and was able to fund them from scholarships and awards. The lessons had to be occasional because Milstein charged £80 per lesson, at a time when well-known British performers, such as the pianists who gave me occasional lessons, might charge between £5 and £10. I remember thinking that the £80 was almost a 'deterrent' set deliberately high to keep most would-be students at bay. My friend asked me if I would come to London to play the piano for his lessons with Milstein. For me, there was no money involved; I just did it for the experience. When I heard what the lessons were costing, I was speechless. Of course, Milstein was a legendary violinist, but still …! According to a historical inflation rate calculator, £80 in the 1970s was the equivalent of today's £872, a sum which will indicate to readers how stunning a fee it was for a single lesson. My friend thought it was worth it to spend a couple of hours in the presence of his hero, especially as Milstein was in the habit of 'playing along' with him, standing right beside him and playing the piece simultaneously. I wasn't sure that constituted 'teaching', but my friend said it was actually very instructive because he could see close up what Milstein was doing, how he moved his hands on the violin and bow, how much pressure he applied, how much effort (or, more precisely, balance of forces) went into producing that famous tone, and even how he breathed. My friend said he would rather learn by observation and osmosis than by being told things in words – and for a talented student with an already advanced technique, this can certainly be a good way to learn.

Milstein was one of those who made it look easy, which was actually instructive in itself. He had a curious habit of 'embroidering' the melody with an improvised descant as the student played, whizzing up and down the violin fingerboard with very quiet flourishes and arpeggios derived from the relevant harmonies, as I imagine Paganini might have done. It was almost as if playing the original melody wasn't enough to occupy his attention. Sitting at the piano, I drank it all in. We made our way through sonata after sonata, Milstein playing along with us, me relishing the superb fragrance of his aftershave, and the young violinist trying to sense what it was like to be him, so that he could internalise that feeling and keep it safe. Money was not mentioned, but it had been conveyed to my friend that he should leave the fee in an envelope on the hall table under the housekeeper's gaze. It was such a large sum that I used to think it was almost meaningless. My friend said that for him, playing to Milstein and spending an hour or two in his company was 'beyond price', but I couldn't help thinking that if it was really beyond price then the great violinist might just as well have charged nothing. It was very hard to see any demonstrable relationship between what was paid and what was given. Was there, perhaps, a temptation to tell oneself that the lesson had been unusually useful because the fee was unusually high? This is not to deny that the lessons were very valuable. My friend considered them a unique privilege. Who is to put a price on the experience of working with someone you revere? Magic can certainly rub off on you. But I couldn't help thinking that the lesson would have been just as interesting for a more compassionate fee.

Sometimes you find yourself in a kind of reverse-Stigwell situation where, even though a pupil is paying you, you have to put it to them that they are mistaken. Arnold came to me full of pride in a system he had worked out over a long period of time. Having found piano technique 'a slippery customer', he had decided to be scientific about it. With the aid of anatomy charts and physics textbooks he had devised a theory of how each finger should relate to the piano keys and how much 'twist' of the individual fingers would be ideal when playing chords. The method was very detailed and a faint memory of Dudley Moore's Mr Stigwell was evoked by Arnold's claim that black notes have 'a different tone' from white notes. When I asked why he thought so, he explained that it was because the lever (which starts at the key and extends into the piano mechanism where it activates the hammer to strike the string) is shorter on the black notes. (It is true that the black keys are shorter than the white, but this is compensated for by weighting of the keys.) He asked me if I had noticed that black keys have a different tone, and he demonstrated the 'different tone' to me. I said that they only had a different tone because he was playing them in a different way, but he disagreed, saying that he had worked it out from scientific principles.

Using this method, he had taught himself a Bach fugue in which the elevation and angle of each finger had been meticulously worked out so that no finger was ever subjected to the shock of random positioning. He knew in advance just how and where each finger would be put down on the key. Unsurprisingly, it had taken him months to learn the Bach fugue in this way. He played it to me. What came across most strongly was his intense concentration on his self-imposed task. While I could sense that nothing had been left to chance, it was also remarkably dull. It was as if, in the effort to construct an anatomical ballet, he had forgotten the music. As I listened to his Bach fugue the image came to me of a series of paving-stones laid carefully next to one another over a lawn, with blades of grass trying to find a way through the cracks.

Not long ago a university student came for a trial lesson with me. She had just arrived in the city to take a postgraduate music degree and was looking for a piano teacher. She played me the slow movement of a sonata by Mozart. All the notes were careful and correct, but the music didn't jump off the page. By that I mean that its spirit remained hidden from me. She gave an equal emphasis to every beat, and an equal energy to every phrase, not distinguishing between beginning, middle and end. I spent an hour working with her on the shape of the movement – its innocent beginning, the deepening complication, the questions posed by the high point, the meaning of the resolution, and the beauty of the little 'coda' tacked on to the end. I spoke about the bars where the texture is simple and open, the other bars where the notes are densely packed together, and what this means in terms of pressure of musical thought.

At the end, I felt that we had made some progress, and I asked her if the lesson had been useful. She paused, looking away, as if searching for a polite form of words, and then said, 'I was hoping you would tell me which muscle groups to use.'

This was a surprise. My heart sank because knowledge of anatomy is not my strong point, and nor was it ever really mentioned by my teachers. I am not sure I could analyse 'muscle groups' – which is not to say that I am not using my muscles in a very precise way. I know I do use my muscles skilfully, but I would not know exactly *which* muscles I use for any given musical task. Perhaps this is part of some pianistic educations, but it hasn't been part of mine, and I can't say I have felt the need to know theoretically what I have already discovered in practice.

I asked her why she would like to know about muscle groups. She said, 'I don't know how to use the weight of my hands and arms on the keyboard.'

'Do you cook? Do you know how to chop things? Do you know how to hammer a nail into a wall?' I asked. 'Yes', she said. 'Do you ride a bike?' 'Yes.' 'Do you know what muscle groups you use when you're doing that?' 'No', she admitted. I pointed out that there are many actions we know from experience how to do, even if we don't know what muscles we're using. There are a million everyday situations in which we have to use the weight of our hands and arms, and we know how to do so. I told her it should be just the same with playing the piano. I asked her if she would know how to bring her fist down on a table if she was angry. She laughed and said 'of course', miming the action perfectly. Would she know how to put in dots for eyes on a tiny cartoon person, using the tip of a fine paintbrush? Would she know how to brush the crumbs off a tablecloth with a gentle lateral movement? Again, she said yes. It's just the same with the piano, I told her. The use of weight is exactly the same, nothing weird or wonderful. There's no special *piano-related* use of weight divorced from the myriad other everyday uses. It may have to be more sensitively calibrated for the piano, but it's the same kind of weight.

'It's important to have a healthy attitude to playing the piano', I told her. 'When you play the piano you don't become a different person with a different body. You are the same person who knows how to use your muscles when you leave this house and ride your bicycle home. And when you play music I don't want you to think consciously of which muscles you're using. I want you to feel what the music is trying to say.'

I tried to explain that we couldn't begin to discuss muscle groups in isolation. First, we would have to know what we wanted to use our muscles *for*. What musical result were we trying to achieve? That was the crucial thing. For example, if she told me she wanted to make a featherlight sound in a certain place in the music, we could discuss how to keep weight out of the piano keys. If she wanted to make a huge loud sound, we could discuss how. When we knew what emotions she wanted to express, we could examine posture and body language and discuss what would best bring about the result she intended. But there was no point in discussing muscle groups without knowing the musical point of using them. For a start, if I went through the piece she had brought me, identifying which muscle groups were to be used where, it would 'fix' her approach in a rigid way, preventing it from changing.

Why was it important to be able to change? Because she would find that at different times, on different days, at various periods of her life, different things in the music would strike her as beautiful or significant. Even its basic character or mood might appear to alter. Our understanding of music goes somehow in tandem with our ability to understand other aspects of life. There would be no point in 'fixing' her way of playing a piece of great music, because it would present different faces to her in different chapters of her life, and it was important to be open to change.

I suppose I shouldn't be surprised how often physical processes become the main focus of a student's mind to the exclusion of musical matters, because when playing music there is a lot to think about besides music. I also give thought to hand and finger positions when I play the piano, but I try to be guided by what I feel the music wants to express, which means that my hand positions are unpredictable, and minutely responsive to the music. Nobody would be able to discern my 'method' without knowing what piece I was playing.

One might think that devising a method of finger placement and the appropriate use of muscles is a good project if its aim is to banish discomfort in the hands and other physical problems. However, experience has shown me that there is a delicate and not straightforward relationship between music and therapies which focus on 'lack of strain'. I have myself taken occasional lessons in Alexander Technique when I have been struggling with a specific physical stress, and over the years many of my colleagues have committed to long periods of regular Alexander sessions, which teach 'optimum balance, posture and co-ordination' as well as how to 'organise yourself with maximum efficiency to optimise your performance in work and everyday life'. Such a goal is of course admirable. I found my own sessions very helpful, though I was never drawn to continue on a regular basis. My colleagues who invested in long-term sessions were delighted to learn how to handle their bodies so that they were better equipped to deal with the unusual twists and torques of playing musical instruments. They learned how to 'push away stress'.

Sometimes, however, I contemplated them in their post-therapy phase of 'playing without strain' and found myself batting away a sneaking feeling that they had surrendered some musical expressiveness as a result. Playing a musical instrument, or more specifically, making music on an instrument is more than just an anatomically correct use of balance and force. Every musician can benefit from understanding good posture. But if musicians prioritise a palette of movements and gestures whose main goals are to be balanced and comfortable, something can be lost in the process because music is 'about' much more than positivity and ease. It may be possible to express its more complex, dark or painful emotions and communicate them to an audience with perfect balance and an attitude which repels stress, but it would be a rare musician who could do so. Naturally one cannot wish for any musician to deny themselves the benefits of physical therapy, but I think we must acknowledge that there isn't a totally simple relationship between 'right use of the body' and musical power.

The human hand is asymmetrical, and composers have always acknowledged this and used it in their music. Pianists spend ages thinking about fingering because different fingers have different strengths. If you want one note to stick out more than another, you can achieve that most easily by choosing a stronger finger (or the thumb) to play it. The index finger is stronger than the little finger, and each has its role to play in creating emphasis, or avoidance of emphasis. Evenness and unevenness both have their expressive importance. You just have to watch a good jazz pianist to see the delightfully uneven 'pairs' of notes they use in fast runs, and the fingering they use to promote that effect known in the French

Baroque period as 'notes inégales'. If you want to bring out details of phrasing, you can choose which fingers to use so that natural strength and weakness of the hand is aligned with the shape and meaning of the phrase. If ever a piano-playing robot could be devised, the inventors would actually have to factor in the unevenness of the human hand, because only then would it sound 'realistic'.

These days it is all too easy to find computer renditions of piano music on the internet. They treat every note as if it were played by the same finger all the time. Each phrase has implacable rigidity; every minim, crotchet and quaver (or half-note, quarter-note and eighth-note) is mathematically the same as every other, allowing no natural 'rubato'. I've been told that enthusiasts sometimes provide these computer versions simply to allow others to hear what the music is like if they do not know it. But the robotic result can suck out all the musicality. If a person did not know the piece already, they would have no reason to love it on hearing it played by a computer. No doubt there are complex programmes to inject 'expression' into computer-generated music, for example to match exciting moments in a film it is accompanying, but the effect is often diluted and even negated by the unnatural sound of computer-generated instruments. It makes one realise how much of music is tied to our natural breathing and physicality, and, indeed, how much of music lies beyond the notes.

And yet it is very common to find people who are attached to playing instruments partly because they represent a complex system, one that is satisfying to master. Their daily practice becomes a goal in itself, and the time they put in can sometimes be confused with active music-making (we're all guilty of it at times). People think that if they spend an hour at the piano they have done an hour's worth of work, and they may indeed have done a pleasurable hour of physical co-ordination. But we cannot take it for granted that when we are playing our instrument we are always making music, and we should learn to notice the difference. Music can fade into the background as we grapple with the writing in of fingering, the geography of the keyboard or fingerboard, the intricacy of notation, the physics of playing the notes, or the thousand and one peripheral things that go into making a performance –administration, rehearsals, concert clothes, the social aspect of getting along with other musicians. Perhaps one could say the same of any art or religious practice whose ultimate goal is so big that it is easier to focus on the component steps and the little organisational tasks that cluster around it, or to tell ourselves that if we put in the time, we must be achieving something meaningful. We should all learn to guard against 'mistaking the pointing finger for the moon', as they say in Zen, because music offers much more and can take us to places we might never glimpse if we remain preoccupied with our love of systems. Playing the piano is a collection of tasks, but even if we diligently attend to the tasks it doesn't mean we are attending to the *music*.

'For me this is like jazz'

Marko, a postgraduate pianist, came for a lesson on Debussy. I was shocked by how inaccurate his playing of the piece was. Not only were the rhythms and rests all over the place, but there were many wrong notes, and he ignored most of Debussy's expression marks. I was puzzled because his piano technique was fluent, and he had a confident air. Could he be dyslexic, I wondered?

'There are a few things we need to check before we talk about the music', I said. 'Let's go through it slowly.'

We started off and I stopped him whenever he was being inattentive to the notation, which was often. After only a page or so he said in irritation, 'I think I have a different feeling about this music.'

'What sort of different feeling?' I asked.

'For me this is like jazz', he replied.

I thought this was promising, because indeed Debussy's music does have jazzy elements. 'Well, I kind of agree with you there', I said. 'Which bits make you think of jazz?'

He looked annoyed. 'I don't think there are specific bits that are like jazz', he said. 'I mean that I don't think Debussy meant his notes to be taken so seriously. For me the notes are just a guideline, a sort of suggestion, like in jazz.'

'Do you mean that Debussy didn't care whether you played his music accurately or not?' I asked.

'Something like that', he said. 'I just think that Debussy wants me to feel free.'

'If Debussy wanted you to "feel free", why did he take the trouble to write all these detailed instructions – all these notes, rests, legato and staccato marks, and expression marks?' I asked.

He shrugged. 'He has to write *something*', he replied. 'But it is just a suggestion. He is a modern composer.'

'You misunderstand Debussy', I told him. 'Has it occurred to you that Debussy has already *written in* the freedoms – the space around the notes, the speeding up and slowing down – that he wants? Debussy calculated his musical effects very carefully. You are not allowed to "feel free" until you have learned to play what he wrote. You can't *start* by feeling free!'

Now Marko understood that I was cross with him, so he stayed silent.

'It's not so much that *you* should feel free as that Debussy's music should *seem free*', I said. And that can only be done by respecting his notation. You don't yet know how this piece is supposed to sound because you haven't bothered to learn the notes. So please do that, and when you know the music, you can tell me if you still feel the need to be free.'

'OK', he said, 'but you are speaking as if this is a piece by Beethoven or something.'

'It *is* a piece by Beethoven or something', I said. 'The something is Debussy.'

Christopher Small in his fascinating book, *Musicking*, discusses the relationship between composer and performer over the centuries, and the responsibility that the one has to the other. His discussion starts from what he sees as a fundamental principle. Music, he writes, 'isn't symphonies or concertos or opera or lieder or pop songs; it isn't even melodies or rhythms. It's an action: it's something people do. All those music objects are to be understood as concretions of the human activity, and it is as activity first and foremost that we need to understand music.' So, if music is primarily an 'activity', and it is the job of the composer to give musicians something to perform, what is the responsibility of the performer faced with a composer's score?

Throughout musical history there have been changing views on where the player, the performer and the composer belong in the hierarchy of who's important. For some communities there aren't even 'performers' in the sense that we know them – just community music-making in which everyone is playing or singing rather than 'performing'. At the other end of the spectrum we find the celebrity performer, and the composer whose texts are practically sacred. In between are examples of times and places where players were encouraged to improvise bits and pieces in composed music. Round about the time of Beethoven, we start to read of composers getting upset if performers tampered with their music, and between then and now the composer's musical text has been of paramount importance to certain kinds of music.

Beethoven himself was a brilliant improviser, yet he hated hearing other pianists taking liberties with his own piano music. Improvisation had its place, but its place wasn't in works of music carefully notated. Other pianists of the day might intersperse 'composed music' with fun improvisations in their concerts. But gradually the habits of improvising faded from classical concerts, while respect for the musical text became ingrained. Composers did not consider themselves as merely 'providing something for people to play'; they had an eye on posterity. They wanted their compositions to endure.

Debussy was also a fluent improviser. He would sometimes sit down at the piano after a dinner party and delight his fellow guests by improvising for an hour or so. He loved the quality of improvisation in performance, but preferred it to arise from a natural-sounding delivery of what he had written. The Italian pianist Alfredo Casella remembered that 'Debussy was extremely exacting of the interpreters of his works. Rarely indeed have I seen him fully satisfied with a performance. He detested all the greatly celebrated virtuosi.' 'All I need is a faithful interpreter', Debussy said.

It's difficult to convey the sensation of feeling free through paying close attention to a text. In theatre terms, people often say the greatest performances of classic roles are when an actor follows the script precisely yet makes it feel immediate and real, as if it is arising in the moment and on the spot. The same is true in music. Being absolutely faithful to the text can be surprisingly liberating. Of course there is no reason why Marko couldn't have done a re-working of Debussy and called it something else, perhaps a jazz piece 'based on an idea by Claude Debussy'. His re-interpretation might have been good, or not. But it wouldn't have been Debussy.

Is playing the notes enough to reveal the music?

Edward, who had come once or twice before for a lesson, had probably been playing the piano for fifty years. He was a very enthusiastic amateur who played every day, had a huge record collection and went to loads of concerts, but had never aspired to performing in public. I knew he loved music from the way he spoke about it, but his love for it didn't come through when he played.

He brought the same volume of music he had brought to the previous lesson, commenting that he would like to have another look at it because he 'wasn't sure what wasn't liked last time'.

I found that an interesting way of putting it. It sounded curiously passive, as though the liking or not liking was a power vested in the teacher, not a power that he himself possessed. '"*What wasn't liked*"?' I said to him. 'Let me pass the ball back to you by asking you whether *you* like the way you are playing it?' 'Well, *I* don't know', he said. 'I hope you're going to tell me if it's good or not.'

I told him I felt uncomfortable with the idea that he was withholding judgement on how things were going. I could tell him my opinion, I said, but it wouldn't necessarily help him when he was next playing the piano on his own. The one who was doing the liking or not liking should, at least in the first instance, be him. To achieve that, he needed to have a sense of what he was aiming at when he played, so that there was something to like (or not).

We started off. He played the first page of a Haydn sonata. It was heavy and plodding. He gave a thump on the beginning of every bar, and kept the pedal down through the rests, so that chords resonated when there was supposed to be silence. The whole thing sounded as if it was made of uncooked dough.

'Let's talk about the character of this music', I suggested. 'What character would you say this has?'

'Playful, lively, comfortable', he said, 'and witty too.' 'I agree!' I said. 'But that's not what I'm hearing when you play it. It sounds heavy and solid.' I leaned over and played the opening of the piece just as he had played it, not even exaggerating for effect.

'That's what it sounds like?' he said with surprise.

'Yes, it does, to be honest. At least it does to me', I said. 'When I ask you what you think about it, all the things you say are good. I feel you understand it well. But there seems to be a gap between what you think about it and what you actually do when you play it. I feel you become obsessed with just getting around the keyboard, and you forget to think about what someone else might be hearing.'

'Are you not hearing lively and playful then?' he asked with a perplexed frown.

'No, I'm actually not', I said. 'That's what I think we should work on in this lesson. It would be great if you could develop the ability to step outside yourself and hear what you're doing. That would be a big step forward.'

'But ...', he said, '... if the music is lively and playful, why are you not hearing that when I play it?'

This was an important question. He had touched on a big subject, one that gives trouble to a great many musicians, especially those unused to performing. People often seem to think that if they simply play the notes correctly, the inner shape and life will come out by themselves. Very occasionally this is true, but in general the player has to assume responsibility for creating an amalgam of the music and their own understanding of it. If they don't realise that they are the agent by which the music becomes acoustically active, the shape and character of the music may remain latent. When I hear this kind of playing I sometimes feel as if someone had made a pile of sand on the beach and then told me proudly, 'I have built a castle'. They *could* build a castle from the pile of sand, but they have to *do it*.

When I complain that students aren't doing this or that, they very often say, 'But I thought I was!' If they are not accustomed to performing, or haven't developed the critical ability to perceive their own playing objectively, they find it difficult to believe that something in their head has not made it into their actual playing. It is possible, of course, to take a piece of music and read it silently to yourself, trying to imagine the music in your head. Some people are really good at this, while others find it very hard indeed. I had a university tutor, Philip Radcliffe, whom I sometimes saw with his nose in a score and a blissful expression on his face which made it perfectly clear to me that he was enjoying the mental music as he read from line to line. The fact that there was *no sound* was immaterial to him: he could imagine the sound. It was evident that he could enjoy reading a score as much as hearing an actual performance, and indeed when I saw him in the audience at our student concerts with the same blissful expression on his face, I wondered if he had actually noticed the sound we were making or whether he was merely using the occasion to activate an ideal sound picture in his head. He never commented on the success or otherwise of our performances, nor on any particular player's ability. Though he did often come backstage to speak to us after concerts, it was invariably to say something along the lines of, 'What marvellous music that is!' He had developed to a remarkable extent the facility of hearing a score in his head. However, when I suggest to students that they should spend time away from the piano, just reading the music and imagining how the piece might go, many of them declare that such an exercise is beyond them. Edward, for example, had told me that when he looked at a score he could only 'hear' it if he had previously heard it being played in reality. If the music was new to him, he could not 'hear' it at all merely by following the score. It naturally follows from this that without such a skill, he – or anyone else in the same boat – would find it nearly impossible to make an interpretative plan away from the piano.

One of the good things about silently reading the score is that it frees you to imagine the music without also having to worry about the geography of the instrument. It also frees you from having to consider the means by which you would make the 'story' of the music come alive for an audience. Silent reading can be enjoyable because it is not a performance art. Playing the piano for one's own private pleasure is also not a performance art, and people get so used to playing in that mode that they don't ask themselves what might need to change if other people are listening. If they have a good intellectual understanding of the music, they often seem to think that this will automatically come through in their playing.

As soon as you invite someone else to listen, however, even if it's just a small group of sympathetic friends, it does cross over into being a performance art. I don't mean that people should start to show off or act unnaturally when they play for others, but I do mean that they ought to cultivate an awareness of what another person is hearing. I am so used to performing that when I play, even for myself, I can't help 'throwing my awareness' outside of myself to include the imaginary listener. I've become attuned to the idea that if I want people to understand the nature of the music, I must bring it to life in my playing, because nobody can look inside my head and enjoy the 'silent image' I have of the score. People who don't aspire to perform often seem unaware of the extent to which it is 'up to them' to make the music real. No student has ever said this to me in so many words, but I often feel they think that if the music *is* passionate, sad, humorous or whatever, then those qualities will be made manifest simply by playing the notes.

Yet the same people wouldn't dream of reading a poem out

loud without trying to convey the poem's effect. They would not drone out, 'How do I love thee? Let me count the ways' in a dreary monotone as if it were a shopping list. Nor would they ever read a fairy story to their children or grandchildren without instinctively using the rise and fall of their voice to make the words jump off the page. Someone might read a story silently to themselves without wondering in what voice the principal characters might speak, but when they read the story to someone else they become 'performers' and make instinctive decisions about pitch, volume, style and pacing. Without those inflections, lines of prose or poetry when read aloud will be inert – and it's just the same in music.

There is another category of people who know what they'd like to do but can't bring themselves to do it, because of shyness or because of cultural constraints. Their imaginations are not idle, but self-consciousness prevents them from acting upon their imaginative schemes. Most of us can remember occasions at school when we were called upon to read out something we loved, and we did it really boringly in order not to draw attention to ourselves. I recall a friend of mine whose school class was the despair of their French teacher because none of them was willing to speak French in a French-sounding way. One day, the French teacher passed through the school's language lab when it was nearly empty and noticed my friend seated at a computer with a pair of headphones on, doing a French-speaking exercise and sounding every inch the Frenchman. The teacher tapped him on the shoulder and asked with amazement, 'Why on earth don't you speak like that in class?' 'You must be joking!' said my friend. 'I'd get beaten up!' In the music world too there seem to be a number of societal reasons – peer pressure, cultural expectations – why people play less well than they could. They sometimes know perfectly well how they would *like* to play, only they're not prepared to do it. With these students the challenge is to persuade them that there are other types of audience with more open minds, audiences who will not sneer at them for artistic aptitude but will welcome what they have to offer.

There's an even more complicated type of student who plays less well than they could because they don't want to face up to the consequences of playing well, such as having to take it seriously and make a commitment, or compete with other talented young musicians. If they don't try their best, they will never find out what their limits are, and it is pleasing to imagine that you *could* be better than everybody if you only tried. When I was a teenager, I knew several such people. As a teacher of advanced students I tend not to come across them any more, because they have either dropped out of the music scene or have seized their destiny and entered with resolve upon the task of being a professional musician.

'Let's speak about the first page of this', I said to Edward. 'Here's a little phrase we might say is a cheeky remark, and then another little phrase which we might say is a soft answer to the remark. Then it all happens again, a bit higher in pitch. Going higher builds up a bit more energy. It spills over into a run of excitable semiquavers, and the phrase ends with a graceful little bow. Let's think of it as one single arch-shaped span from the first bar to the twelfth.' I leaned over and demonstrated the whole phrase in the top octaves of the keyboard.

'Oh yes, it is one big phrase, isn't it?' he said. 'I hadn't noticed that.' He copied me while it was still fresh in his mind. 'Ah, that's much better!' he said.

We moved on to the next passage. 'Now the excitable semiquavers stop, and a smooth movement of even quavers takes over', I said. 'It's a contrast in texture and in mood. And again the phrase rises up in pitch. It stays smooth, but it does become more intense. And how? Because of the harmonies, which start off in the home key, but gradually turn to C minor, which is a harder sound, and then octaves are added in the bass, to thicken the texture. So the rhythm stays even, but the feeling of pressure increases because the pitch rises and the harmonies change. Then we have three little phrases which seem to be attempting to reach a close of some kind. The first two don't manage it, but the third one does reach a half-close on a seventh chord of F. Do you see how the last bars have this lovely line in the left hand passing from G through G flat to F where it comes to rest? It's like a note of regret, another colour passing briefly through the music, would you say?'

Edward was pleased with this sketch. I demonstrated it; he copied me, and was pleased with the effect. 'It makes the whole passage seem shorter', he commented. This was very gratifying because it showed he had been able to 'seize' the various elements together in his mind. 'I like this way of doing it', he said. 'Now it seems like we've had two big phrases instead of just twenty-odd bars.' He played the whole thing from the beginning. It was very much better, and I told him so. Nothing had changed in his piano-playing technique, but I as a listener was more carried along, because I felt he had been following an *imaginative scheme*.

I was left wondering what had been going through his head during the long period when he had been playing the piece on his own. Had he simply been playing the notes over and over again, absorbed in the physical challenge? Playing the piano is a physical process, satisfying in its own right, but a piece of music is not just a length of the swimming pool. Instrumental playing has things in common with sport: it's an enjoyable physical challenge of co-ordination, spatial awareness, accuracy, speed and stamina. But if that's what you want, you could get the same satisfaction from tennis, golf or football. Instrumentalists can't make beautiful music without mastering the physical task, but the physical task is only the gateway to an imaginative world. Unless the musician engages with that world, music will remain a series of patterns, restricted in what they can communicate. Lots of players seem content to play the patterns, but such playing will never move an audience. This is the great challenge of playing an instrument, particularly one as complicated as the piano: to master the physics well enough that we are free to pay attention to the language.

To sway or not to sway

Anton was an excellent young professional pianist who came for a lesson on Brahms. When he played, he swayed around mightily, moving not only backwards and forwards but also left and right. He was a tall and willowy person, so the circle of his movement was large and very distracting to watch. Sometimes he almost writhed as he played, like someone in pain. I found myself thinking how remarkable it was that he could actually keep playing the notes when his centre of gravity was changing all the time.

It reminded me of a moment in Sándor Végh's violin class in Prussia Cove when Végh made everyone laugh by teasing a violinist who kept changing the angle of the violin as she played. Sometimes the violin was parallel to the ceiling and then suddenly almost parallel to the wall. As the violinist moved the violin around, she had to keep adjusting her bowing arm and her posture. Végh wagged his finger at her and said, 'Imagine you are a pianist playing a piano which keeps changing its position. One moment the keyboard is here; the next moment it is here!' he said, miming the reaction of a poor seasick pianist as an imaginary keyboard tipped rakishly to one side. 'If the piano keyboard kept moving around, pianists would never feel safe!' he said. 'It is one of the great things about the piano that its position is fixed. Pianists know where the keyboard is going to be. And the position of the violin can be reliable too. Find the best position to apply the weight of the bow to the violin. Don't keep changing the angle!'

Obviously Anton was not able to change the angle of the piano keyboard, but he was constantly changing the angle of his own body in relation to the piano keys, which made things almost as difficult. You didn't need to be a physicist to see that when he leaned far back on the piano stool he was putting himself at a disadvantage because he was using so much energy to hold his spine in an unnatural position.

He was not alone in compromising his piano technique with 'expressive' body language. We all do it at times. I felt I knew where the impulse came from: it was a way of showing involvement, expressing the twists and turns he found in the music. To sit still and show nothing would have felt cold and detached. He was trying to demonstrate on the outside what he felt on the inside. Yet all the moving about was actually making his life more difficult. More significantly, it wasn't doing anything to help the sound.

'If I was listening to you on a recording', I said to him, 'I wouldn't be able to see any of this "expressive" movement. All I would hear is the sound. So: save your energy for doing things which influence the sound. When you move around so much, you're reducing the control you have over the keys. It's the way you touch or strike the keys which makes the sound. If I was sitting in a concert hall watching you,' I said, 'I might be able to add the visuals to what I heard, to make a sort of "combined artwork" of your playing. But many people won't be watching you when they hear you play. They'll be listening on their phones or tablets or radios. They won't see your expressive movements. So you should focus on how to affect the sound, because your sound is the "signature" that will always represent you.'

'Play that page again and try to keep still', I said. 'I don't mean stiff. I mean physically calm. Think of Rachmaninov! A brilliant pianist who sat very still when he played.'

Anton played the page again. I could see he was putting effort into not moving. 'Now I feel I must look as if I don't feel *anything* for the music', he complained. 'What is wrong with moving around? People like to watch the movements. You spoke about listening to music on your phone, but you know you can watch people on your phone as well. People might be watching my performances on YouTube!'

It flashed through my mind that he and I were approaching this from different vantage-points. He had grown up in an era in which image was crucial in some kinds of musical career where sheer ability was sometimes a secondary matter. I on the other hand had been taught to think that it was in bad taste to devote too much attention to your appearance. When I was growing up, a record was always released without accompanying visuals, but for Anton's generation, 'the music video' excited people almost more than the song. In the pop world, famous film directors were given enormous budgets to shoot these music videos, sometimes with hundreds of people in the cast. Even in the world of classical music, artists' publicity was getting steadily more sophisticated, and the younger the musicians were, the more comfortable they seemed to be with manipulating the media. Was I entitled to tell a young pianist that visual effect was beside the point? I had said, 'Think of Rachmaninov', because he was an example of someone who didn't show off. That appealed to me. When I thought of my own pianistic icons, they tended to have restrained platform manners. But what about pianists in other eras – such as Liszt? I bet he swayed about and gazed into the stratosphere. What about Beethoven and Mozart? Did they writhe and make painful faces to entertain their listeners? I could imagine they put on their best shiny clothes and shoes to perform, but I had read nothing to indicate that they 'chewed the scenery' when they played in public.

Irrespective of passing fashions in performance style, pianists have probably always divided into those who consciously used body language to charm their audiences, and those who just concentrated on the music. It was probably at least as much a matter of individual temperament as of historical era. At any rate, I was convinced that focusing on the music was the only course that had enduring value. I wasn't really interested in commenting on a student's body language unless I felt it was causing technical problems or getting in the way of the music. No composers (except possibly someone eccentric like Erik Satie) ever gave instructions on how to behave physically as you play the music – their requests are all to do with how the music is to *sound*. It seemed clear that great composers weren't interested in prescribing the gyrations a performer should make. They never write, 'Hunch forward here and let your head droop until your nose is almost touching the keys', or 'Toss your hair now and put on a tragic expression for the next eight bars'. All of that comes into the realm of 'how to put it across', an infinitely flexible matter on which composers are wisely silent. All the choreographic stuff is transient. Setting it aside, we pianists have only a fixed keyboard and a musical score to bring to life as sound. For us, the crux of the matter is the point at which the finger meets the piano key. This small area and none other is the point where we can actually be *effective*. It's our equivalent of the place where the violin bow meets the string, the place where the actual work is done.

They say you should 'dance as if nobody's watching', but I believe you should play as if the dance were in the sound.

How important is it to hear the sound?

A while ago I had an enquiry from someone who wanted to come and have a piano lesson. He explained that I might not want to teach him when I heard about his situation. He was an advanced pianist, but he now suffered from an array of hearing problems. Not only was he deaf in the ordinary sense, but he could no longer hear pitches accurately. Sometimes he heard notes as 'double pitches'. Sometimes he heard a note as one thing in the left ear, and another note in the right ear. Sometimes he could not distinguish pitches at all. He told me that listening to music had become a torture because it was just a cacophony. He had stopped going to concerts entirely, even to support friends who were performing, because it was so unpleasant to sit there and not recognise the piece they were playing. He could not listen to the radio. His sense of pitch had become so distorted that instrumental music often seemed more like white noise.

Nevertheless, he said, he still enjoyed playing the piano and would like to come and have a lesson on a Beethoven sonata.

I had never come across such a case before – at least, I had never heard of someone who still wanted to have a music lesson even though they could no longer hear the music. I was not unfamiliar with the link between pianists and deafness. Many pianists, including me, suffer from some high-frequency hearing loss, which may be associated with years of practising pianos in small rooms. An audiologist had once told me that I would be surprised if I knew how many well-known pianists, and in fact instrumentalists of all kinds, still manage to continue their careers despite some playing-related hearing loss. But I had never heard of anyone who wanted to keep playing and even having piano lessons when listening to music had become 'a cacophony'. To be honest, I rather dreaded the effect that the cacophony might have on his playing. I wasn't sure if I could say anything worthwhile in the circumstances, but I said he should come and play to me and we'd see if there was something we could work on.

He came along and played me his Beethoven sonata, and I was amazed. First of all, his actual sound was better than that of many of my other 'hearing' students. It was thoughtful and warm. He played accurately and with feeling. In fact, he almost never played a wrong note. I couldn't believe he wasn't able to hear what he was doing, but he assured me he couldn't. 'For example,' he said, choosing two notes quite widely spaced apart on the keyboard, 'if you were to play me these two notes one after the other and ask me which one is higher, I wouldn't know.'

'So how are you doing this?' I wondered.

'I learned to play this piece when I was a boy', he said, 'and the physical patterns are still in my memory. I know what it *should* sound like. I can imagine the music while I play. But I have no idea what it sounds like in the room. I don't know what you are hearing.'

'Could you learn a new piece of piano music?' I asked. 'Certainly not', he answered. 'I can only imagine something that I got to know when my hearing was normal. If I tried to learn something new, I would just be looking at the notation and putting my fingers on the keys without really being able to make a link between the two things. I wouldn't know what sounds I was playing, so I wouldn't be able to form an idea of a new piece. I don't score-read well enough to be able to imagine the sound of something that I've never heard being played.'

'But you've told me that music sounds more or less like white noise', I said. 'Is it really possible for you to play this Beethoven sonata and "hear it" without being horribly distracted by the jumble of pitches you've told me about? I can't begin to imagine how difficult that must be.'

'Well', he said sadly. 'I have no alternative, do I? I still love the physical sensation of playing the piano. If it's a piece I've known for a long time, like this one, I can somehow superimpose a memory of it on the cacophony that I actually hear. It's hard, though. I've been told', he said with a small smile, 'that most people who have my type of hearing problems just give up playing altogether.' 'I'm not surprised', I said. 'I don't think I could do what you can do. You must have unbelievable will-power.'

During the lesson I demonstrated things on the piano, as I usually do. It was strange to think that my student could not hear me, or not in the way that I would have hoped, but he responded to the demonstrations as constructively as a student with normal hearing would do. He seemed to be watching my hands on the piano and extracting information from what he saw, rather than from what he heard. He must have been working backwards from the end result (my touch on the keys) to the thought or feeling that led me to use those gestures. I was struck once again by how much is possible if you work from the outside in, rather than the inside out.

When I'm teaching I often feel that people are imagining something in their heads, but not managing to transfer those visions into their actual playing. Here was someone who, despite being forced to grapple with cruel pitch distortion, was using his sense of touch, his memory and his musical imagination to play more beautifully than many people do. He seemed to have developed the capacity to go directly from imagination to keyboard without letting his auditory problems get in the way.

The next time I saw him he surprised me by announcing that he wanted to play twelve Chopin Études in a single lesson. I suggested we work on just one or two, but he said that he had set himself the goal of playing all twelve, which he then did. The Chopin Études are full of changing harmonies which shift about with great complexity. He played these chromatic passages very accurately, although it was possible to discern that he was not savouring the changes of key as a person with normal hearing might. Once again I couldn't imagine what motivated him to put in sufficient practice to learn these enormously difficult piano pieces if he couldn't hear the pitches. I asked him, and he replied that of course he could *see* the score and imagine it, even though as time went by his ability to 'hear the harmonies inwardly' was, as he put it, simplifying. As I watched him play I reflected that for me the beauty of Chopin's microscopically sensitive harmonies is one of the chief reasons for working at his piano pieces. If I couldn't hear them, would I have the heart to play them? I doubted it. At the same time, I had the feeling that these passages could be enjoyed purely for their spatial geometry, if I could put it like that. That was what I seemed to see as I watched my student flying about the keyboard. He may not have been savouring the harmonies, but instead he seemed to be tuning in to the poetry of these notes in space.

Music is expressed in sound, but without sound there can still be music. Love of music had given this man the resolve to keep going. Although he was unable to hear his own playing, I could hear it and was happy to assure him that he had succeeded in making music. His case reminded me of the achievements of certain composers, like Fauré and Smetana, who somehow kept composing despite suffering from deafness and tinnitus. I was about to draw a parallel with Beethoven, who composed some of his finest music when he was deaf, but then it occurred to me that Beethoven's case was probably less complicated: he may have suffered from 'a roar in his ears' but, as far as I know, he was not plagued by horrible pitch distortion. Perhaps Beethoven didn't hear much when he played his piano, but at least he was not confronted with a blizzard of nonsense.

After my student had gone, my husband came downstairs and said, 'Was that really the man who can't hear pitches? You really wouldn't know. I thought he played beautifully.'

Truly it seemed a case of mind over matter. I had been apprehensive about teaching this man, but as it turned out, he was an inspiration.

Section Two

Learning

Beethoven among the Alpine flowers

I have already touched on the advantages and dangers of the masterclass. When I was learning to play the piano, all my lessons were individual ones, just the teacher and me. The concept of 'learning in front of an audience of your peers' or 'learning in public' was unknown to me and my friends. The only time we heard one another play was in a competitive music festival or in a concert, and in those forums the concept of 'learning' was not the primary focus.

Not knowing any differently, I was quite happy with my individual music lessons and had become accustomed to the privacy of the setting. If I played well or badly, only the teacher heard it. If my teacher praised me, I had to hug the memory to myself because there was no one to share it with. On the other hand, if my teacher was cross because I had neglected to practise, nobody had to know. Only the lesson notebook might bear witness to what my teacher thought of my progress on a week-to-week basis, but nobody except me ever looked at the notebook and in any case its gnomic comments ('Debussy: count!!' 'Mozart: the *thumb*!') didn't encourage leisure reading.

Of course, the group learning method was familiar to me because of school. Piano lessons (which happened outside of school) were a contrast to the class setting of my school lessons. In a class of thirty-two children I was used to getting only the occasional moment of any teacher's undivided attention and therefore I rather relished the one-to-one 'confessional' of the individual music lesson, where I never had to pluck up courage to put my hand up to ask or answer a question, or indeed to wonder whether it would be wiser not to put my hand up this time, but leave someone else to answer. In music lessons it was good to ask and answer questions.

Until I had finished university, all my instrumental lessons were one-to-one. It was only then, when I began attending postgraduate masterclasses and music courses, that I encountered the European performance class with all its potential for drama.

My first experience of such a class was at the International Musicians' Seminars in Prussia Cove, Cornwall, where I was first a student and later the class pianist for Sándor Végh's violin classes as well as Johannes Goritzki's cello class, William Pleeth's cello class, Bruno Giuranna's viola class, and a number of others over the years. Some professors, perhaps those less accustomed to the performance class format, basically gave the lesson they would have given in private. Ignoring the other listeners as best they could, they focused on the individual student and spoke to him or her without adjusting their manner to the setting. Other professors extended the 'performance' idea to their own teaching, relishing the opportunity that an audience provided.

Every morning in Sándor Végh's class was like a visit to the theatre. He understood instinctively that pedagogical points would spring to life and be remembered for ever if they were delivered in a colourful way. Sometimes this involved larger-than-life praise of the student, but sometimes his criticism could be cruel. The students swallowed the criticism because they so much enjoyed the moments of extravagant praise. Although I as the class pianist was not the one having the lesson, I was nevertheless treated to both praise and censure without restraint. As I was a professional tasked with the job of playing umpteen different piano parts, sometimes with no notice at all, I at first thought it was ridiculous to treat me as fair game for the same kind of criticism meted out to the students. But like them I learned to bite back my feelings because it was so much fun on the admittedly more numerous occasions when Végh roared with satisfaction at something I had done and held me up to the class as a shining example of musicianship. Though I didn't enjoy being criticised, I realised I was actually learning a huge amount about a lot of different repertoire and was, in effect, having a lesson every time one of the students had one.

I encountered the performance class on a larger scale when I spent a semester at the wonderful Banff Centre in Canada. Banff at that time offered visiting scholarships which one could take up for a semester or more, meaning that one's only expense was the cost of getting to Canada. Members of my group Domus, who made up a piano quartet (violin, viola, cello and piano), decided to go to Banff for one winter semester to give ourselves some peace and quiet to rehearse properly and try out new approaches. We auditioned and managed to get scholarships which provided accommodation and food for three months, a delightful luxury. When we got to Banff, I loved my room looking out over the magnificent snowy mountains. In Banff I came across for the first time a system where there were no permanent teachers but rather a rotating list of visiting arts professors who came for a day, a few days, a week at a time. You could sign up to play to any visiting professor, whether in the music faculty or in another department (such as drama or improvisation) if you felt it might be relevant, although you didn't have to play to anyone at all if you were not in the mood for outside intervention. You could tailor-make your own course of study and we decided to play to as many visiting teachers as we could.

This was an extremely interesting process for all of us, because we were used to having teachers whose attitudes were consistent and predictable. When we started playing to the visiting professors, we instantly discovered that each of them had their own views on the merits and otherwise of our playing. They had different recipes for what we needed to do, and their recipes sometimes contradicted those of others. One professor might tell us that our group was too focused towards the string players, while the next might tell us that the piano was too dominant. One professor might say that our style was delightfully European, while the next might compliment us on having transcended our European roots and learned to play in an 'international' style which made sense in North America. One professor might say that we were too solemn, the next that we were too frivolous and spent too much time laughing. Someone might tell us that we were pedantic about the detailed markings in the score, but the next might say that we were relying too much on spur-of-the-moment inspiration and needed to go back to the score and study it better. We might be told that our Brahms was 'too German' and then in the next session that our Brahms was 'not German enough'.

All this was fascinating, and not only because of what we were learning about ourselves. I started to attempt my own psychological evaluation of the visiting professors, trying to guess on which side of the fence their comments would land. Gradually we all realised that each professor came with his or her own set of expectations and values, usually linked to their own educational background, nationality, and personality type. Their advice was not 'absolute' but rather a reflection of their taste, contingent on their own upbringing and experience. Some of the students in Banff (who like us were new to the 'rotating' professorial system) found this very confusing. They were used to being pointed in a particular direction by their teachers and then being guided along that path for years at a time. They wanted advice that would stand them in good stead in all seasons. They didn't know what to make of it when one professor told them they were too inward-looking and the next told them that they needed to look inwards more. It took us all a while to adjust to an environment in which advice changed constantly. We felt a bit like children who get confused and upset by lack of boundaries, and who long for simple guidelines.

We also realised that the professor on a flying visit has a tempting opportunity to 'hit out' at students without having to deal with the consequences. Most tutors were careful not to do this, but occasionally a visiting professor would abuse the power latent in the drama of a performance class. Here again we sensed that there were differences of educational approach in tutors from different parts of the world. It seemed that in some countries – Eastern European for example – it was considered acceptable, even salutary, for a student to be 'taken apart' by a renowned teacher. We in the audience noticed very different responses from the students involved, responses which also differed along national lines. The cutting remark seemed to be more or less taken in their stride by students used to that system. Indeed, they didn't seem to feel it had been a proper lesson if they hadn't been given a few verbal blows or insults. By contrast, US students from an educational system which aims to empower and encourage them by accentuating the positive found it shocking and insulting to be mocked and criticised so overtly. In the delightfully 'can-do' atmosphere of the Banff Centre, where every student was the centre of attention and every performance offered something to praise, negative teaching methods felt horribly jarring. I remember one particular class where a cellist played for cello guru János Starker. The young cellist played with a light-hearted swagger, a nonchalant style and a winning smile which he could usually count on to endear him to audiences. We all knew this wouldn't be to Starker's taste. There was a silence when the young cellist finished playing. Then, after a meaningful pause, Starker said very deliberately, 'Your playing is the kind of playing I have spent years of my life trying to stamp out.' Everyone gasped. It was shockingly un-empowering. The young cellist was, quite understandably, deeply offended and the rest of the lesson passed in barely concealed hostility on both sides. Starker tried to explain that fidelity to the score was his Bible, but he had lost the fruitful moment.

I noticed afterwards that the listeners were divided in their response to Starker's judgement. The student himself was clearly all the more determined to go on playing the way he preferred. He said he would much rather have good communication with audiences than be a living example of fidelity to the score. Plenty of people sympathised. Others felt that although Starker's comments were dreadfully insensitive, even brutal, his advice was actually correct. Still others felt that although his comments were not to be swallowed uncritically, they opened up a viewpoint worth exploring. Again one could see that, depending on each person's cultural attitudes, the question of whether a teacher's word is law or not was interpreted very differently. Is the teacher in the service of the student, or the student in the service of the teacher? Anyone who saw Paul Tortelier's televised masterclasses in the 1980s will probably remember the feeling that the students' problems and foibles were sometimes used by the maestro to point up his brilliance by comparison. For some viewers he went beyond the bounds of the acceptable in remarks such as, 'You play like a virgin. You are a virgin, n'est-ce pas?' Many people loved the drama of his lessons because he was very handsome, had great charisma and was indisputably a terrific cellist. If you simply sat back and relished the drama without wondering what it felt like to be the student, it was enthralling television (as many people said at the time). As pedagogy, however, it was flawed, and today it would raise questions.

Some of the students in Banff gradually decided not to play to every visiting tutor, but to be judicious about whom they played to (which probably meant that they wanted to be confirmed in what they already thought). My colleagues and I went the other way, playing to everyone we could. We had already discovered from our own concerts that every audience is different and that while one group of listeners will take you to their heart, the next may be unresponsive. From our conversations with audience members, we had realised that if you ask ten people for their opinion on your playing, you must brace yourself for ten opinions. In other words, we knew that whether people like you or not depends on them, not on you. In a funny way we felt liberated by an environment in which everyone responded to us differently; it made us realise that we had to develop our own style and believe in it. We had all studied with individual teachers whom we saw week after week and year after year without anything arising to challenge their views. The Banff Centre offered a range of opinions. This made it a stimulating environment, and I felt happy there. In fact, I remember feeling that all the stimulation had caused my mind to work in a higher gear.

In Banff I had my first meeting with the Hungarian piano professor György Sebök (I wrote about this in my 2004 book *Beyond the Notes*). I was looking forward to hearing him teach because Isobel Rolston, director of the music programme at Banff, had said to me with a meaningful look, 'I think you, in particular, will like him'. Here for the first time and to my astonishment I encountered a teacher who seemed to have no 'method' and no agenda, but was, as he said himself, 'a mirror', reflecting back to the student what they were doing. His mission was to find out what each student's musical dreams were and to help them achieve them. Unlike many other teachers, he didn't want to dictate what the dream should be, but was non-judgementally interested to see if the student was succeeding in realising their own dreams. Often there is a gap, he said, between the way that someone would like to play and the way that they actually play. He was interested to help them bridge the gap.

Perhaps it wasn't quite as objective as that, because obviously Sebök had his own dreams and couldn't help being sympathetic to pianists who thought along the same lines as he did. But, given that natural affinity, he was able to appreciate, understand and support an amazingly wide range of playing. Even if he didn't support it, he was interested to know why it was as it was. He was more successful than any other teacher I've encountered at keeping his own musical preferences in the background and focusing on what the student was actually doing. This included their musical approach, their physical attitude at the piano, and their psychological type. He knew that people play music for all sorts of reasons and that some people use music as a way of bolstering their confidence, putting up a smokescreen, or hiding behind the task of music-making so that they didn't have to address other issues in their lives. There were all sorts of reasons – altruistic as well as egocentric – why a person would wish to perform in front of others. The reasons were evident in their playing and in their way of interacting or not interacting with the audience. A person's demeanour at the piano could be read as an expression of their inner world.

I had been used to my teachers talking about music in a certain way. They talked about phrasing, beauty of tone, about the shape of the piece, about correct historical style. They spoke about being careful to observe the composer's instructions. They talked about physical balance and posture, respect for the score and good communication with the audience. They talked about concert dress and platform manner. All of these are good and necessary things to make students aware of. Beyond those things, they didn't really venture, and even though I might have had notions about what might lie 'beyond', I had grown used to the fact that nobody ever put those things into words. When I talk about the things which 'lie beyond', I'm referring to the way that music impacts on us and what cycles of response it sets in motion in us. When you spend a lot of time practising music and listening to it, you become aware of developing subtly nuanced responses. It appeals to you, it strikes you as beautiful, it's touching, it's intellectually intriguing; it may have mathematical interest, fun pattern-making, physical demands. The more that the composer has tried to put into it and succeeded in expressing, the more complex will be the player's response to it. Choice of key and use of harmony and modulation are hugely meaningful for any sensitive player and evoke the most detailed and synaesthetic responses. But music and words are not exact parallels and it is often nearly impossible – or feels nearly impossible – to put into words why something seems important. It's equally difficult to speak about the phases of one's relationship with the instrument and with the discipline of studying music. Day after day you experience the challenge of moving forward, the difficulty of keeping an open heart. You love music, but sometimes it feels as if you might hate it as well. You long to perform, but you'd really rather not. You are desperate to share your passion for music, but you fear that if you share it, it will be somehow spoiled. You want to be heard and appreciated, but you hate it when anyone walks in on your practising. You wonder whether the effort of mastering an instrument is making music feel like work instead of play. How to make it feel like play again? I had grown used to the silence around these questions. These were matters of which one could not speak.

So I was enthralled when Sebök said casually to one of his piano students, 'There are some totally automatic functions in the body and some semi-automatic ones, like breathing. Music-making too is in this semi-automatic category and, like breathing, it is possible to decide not to breathe, to run out of breath and fail to inhale. When you are playing an instrument, you must make sure that music is active. Try to notice when it has become extinct.'

This was a new sort of teaching for me.

'A sound is something you mean', he said in one of those first lessons. 'Don't let your hands be independent of you.'

It was poetic licence to say that 'a sound is something you mean', because obviously you can make a sound without meaning anything in particular – but why would you do so if you are a real musician? It was so simple and yet so illuminating. Were we merely playing the notes in front of us in the score without having any connection to them? Clearly it was possible to do so – one hears it all the time. So what would be involved in 'meaning' a sound? A moment's contemplation made it clear that in order to 'mean' the sound, you would first have had to digest the music, internalise it, make some emotional or intellectual connection with it, or in contemporary parlance 'own it', so that when you set about playing it for other people, it seemed to come from you, or at least *through you*. 'Don't let your hands be independent of you'? Like most other young pianists I had probably spent half my practice time doing things over and over to fix them in my memory. I had even marvelled at my fingers' ability to reproduce the music over and over while I allowed myself to think about something else. It was a kind of circus trick. Now when I confronted the admonition not to let my hands be independent of me, it seemed laughable that I would ever have let them be so. It was so obvious that the 'meaningless sound' was a waste of time.

In an interview published in *The Piano Quarterly* in 1976, Sebök had elaborated on this notion of 'meaning' something when you play. 'I think there is a very big and important difference between truth and lie, but not in the ordinary sense of the word. For example, if I play a phrase the way I mean it, in a muscular and psychological peace with myself, then I told the truth. If my bad physical habits or the shortness of my thumb made me play the phrase another way, then I told a lie, the same kind of lie as a false smile. If only my facial muscles are smiling, then it's a lie. And if only the muscles of my arm are playing the phrase, then it's a lie, too. But I think it should be part of practising to discover the truth, or at least to detect the presence of the lie.'

This quote gives a flavour of his way of speaking, not very different in reality than it comes across in print. It sometimes seemed as though a book was speaking to you, in finely-honed sentences in no need of editing. Obviously Sebök was exceptionally intelligent. He gave the impression of being well-read in many subjects apart from music and being able to draw on a wide range of references. Almost as striking was his self-possession, or to put it another way, his lack of self-doubt. My own experience of teaching is that I constantly wonder if I am saying the right thing or making the right judgement. Sebök never gave that impression. He spoke quietly and calmly, never seeming to be surprised by anything and never appearing to have to search for an appropriate response. He seemed to be ready for anything and yet at the same time not attached to anything. How had this been achieved? His 'life journey' didn't particularly seem to explain it. By his own account he had found teaching came naturally to him since he was a little boy explaining the world to his sister, so it seemed that nature had simply endowed him with unusual powers of judgement and expression.

'Sometimes I say that the player creates time, that musical time without notes in it doesn't exist, like space not existing without matter', he said. 'And sometimes I say that time goes on without you, that you don't have to push it. These are two different images, each of which can be useful in the right moment, like tools from an immense toolbox. But the best of all is to throw both of these images away.'

'When we breathe,' he said, 'we inhale before an important remark. But the depth of inhalation doesn't depend on the length of the sentence; it depends more on the importance of the statement. The more important, the deeper you inhale.' He mimed taking an enormous breath and then saying 'I love you' to the student. Then he took a quick gulp of breath and said 'I love you' again. Although 'I love you' was only three words, it was clear that its emotional import required a long 'upbeat' in the form of breathing in. Not much breath was needed to say three little words, but if the speaker only took a little breath, then the three words sounded trivial. It was astounding. The parallels with music-making were obvious.

'Emotion should precede the notes because if it doesn't, the music just "runs empty"', he said. 'And not just emotion, but *attitude* should precede music. You can't make a gesture and then decide what you meant it to say.'

A cellist came in and played the Bach C minor cello suite for him. They spent some time talking about the Sarabande, a slow and sorrowful movement of the suite. The cellist explained that his method of working on it was to try and find resonances in his own experience, so that he could 'make sense' of the music by comparing it to things he knew about. Sebök smiled and said, 'When you play something as great as the Sarabande, you communicate by experiencing it with great humility. What is there to understand?

If you insist on presenting your own "understanding", you may communicate less than the music has. It is like building a skyscraper and putting the roof on the skyscraper too soon. This is the danger of finding consonances with one's own inner world and presenting the results as "one's own" version of the piece. Maybe you have to be willing to live in a house without a roof.' (These are actual quotes which I noted down at the time, though I missed some sentences because I was still trying to write down his exact wording of the previous one. It seemed important to me at the time to 'get his voice', not just a summary.)

To a viola player he said, 'You put such intensity into short motifs that when I tell you to think in long phrases, it is for you the equivalent of relaxing. But it should not be.'

'Playing the viola is *work* in your mind, and work is always *against* something. Yeats's line, "How can we know the dancer from the dance?" is an answer to almost all questions. If you cannot tell the dancer from the dance, then there is no *work*. There are of course measurable energies being spent, but they are not *work*.'

These examples show several things about his teaching which were important for me. First of all, he dealt in underlying principles. Secondly, he refrained from being personally critical of the student, speaking rather about the effects of their attitude and approach. He seemed to treat music as a form of philosophy. Music for him was not just an arrangement of notes designed to please the ear and while away the time. Rather, it was a kind of symbolic world with which every musician interacted, offering in the process not only an interpretation of the music but a living demonstration of the musician's motives, character and approach to life in general. How a person approached a piece would show things about the piece, but also things about the player. Sebök was interested in how each impacted on the other. Sometimes it seemed that a piece of music would do the player good. Sometimes it seemed that a player would illuminate the piece for the audience's benefit. Someone's limitations might be shown by the way they failed to engage with great music.

On the other hand, a player might be able to demonstrate through music that they had far greater powers of understanding than you might have thought merely by talking to them.

A player might show by their ability to 'open up' a crescendo that they had the ability to open up in life more generally. Someone who knew how to stand respectfully back and let the music speak for itself was a person who understood how to keep their own ego at bay, unless of course they were a person who was hiding behind the composer's confidence. Sebők was very sensitive to the bond created (or not created) between musician and music, and it seemed that there were infinite permutations of students and pieces of music to create a never-ending series of pedagogical points. 'I think that the class situation helps very much', he had told *Piano Quarterly*. 'The privacy of the studio, the tête-à-tête with the student is important too, but the class situation becomes like an accelerator, with a power of its own and a strong kind of feedback. The students in attendance become the public. I usually don't even talk very much to the person who plays, but I explain him to the others.' This remark shows his degree of comfort with the class situation, but also perhaps his detachment from the individual student. Perhaps 'detachment' is the wrong word. He often spoke about the importance of maintaining objective distance as a teacher, and he once remarked that objectivity was not at all the same thing as 'remoteness'. His objectivity was a welcome change to many of us who had been used to a perhaps intrusive degree of control from our previous music teachers. On the other hand, the same objectivity could sometimes make you feel that you were mainly of interest as an opportunity to point out interesting problems and solutions.

I find it very difficult to analyse why this method of teaching so appealed to me. One of the most unusual things about it, in fact, was his ability to find words for things that most people don't try to put into words. I remember him discussing a long crescendo passage at the climax of a Beethoven piano sonata. The pianist played it, demonstratively, as a thunderous climax. Sebők told the student that they should be careful not to confuse 'aurora moments' with threatening moments. 'If you make it dramatic or threatening, it is less powerful', he said quietly. 'This passage is more like the sunrise. There is nothing *personal* about a sunrise.' In a few words he had summoned up a picture which changed everyone's perspective, in a way which felt right for the music.

His sentences rolled out with calm precision (there are some 'clips' of his teaching on YouTube if you want to hear how he spoke). Perhaps he had tried some of them before and honed them in use in other lessons; after all, among students there are certain 'types' one can expect to encounter over and over again. It didn't feel like that, however, because he seemed to be responding so particularly to the student in front of him. I suppose that is why he never wanted to write a book. With his gift for language and analysis he could have written wonderful books, but I suspect he would have regarded any book as a sterile exercise in 'fixing' his views. What interested him was the challenge of coming up with the right response in a 'live' situation. It was almost like a dare that he had given himself, to see if he could 'nail' the situation without any preparation. It made me think of the story he'd told us about when he was a young man and had been given a regular spot to play piano music on Hungarian radio. To make life more interesting, and out of sheer chutzpah, he'd set himself the task of taking an obscure volume of piano music out of the library and not even looking at it until the red light went on in the studio. Then he would open the book at random, sit down at the piano and sight-read the piece on air. (I am a good sight-reader myself, but such audacity would be beyond me.) When he was spending the bulk of his time as a teacher, he still delighted in marshalling his forces on the spur of the moment. It was a kind of performance of its own.

He had a command of English which few native speakers have. I used to think of the Polish novelist Joseph Conrad, who became a master of prose style in the English language and yet brought to it an intriguingly Eastern European sensibility. Sebök was the same. When he spoke English he never seemed to grope for words or intersperse his phrases with 'erm' and 'uh'. On the contrary, his choice of words seemed at times forensically accurate, at other times like poetry. 'When I hear you play,' he told a string-playing friend of mine, 'I have the image of a silkworm excreting silk from its mouth. The silk should be produced effortlessly. In your playing, I feel some resistance: the silk thread has to be *pulled* steadily from the mouth.' We who were listening looked at one another with big eyes to acknowledge not only the justice of this remark, but also its artistry. He had a terrific instinct for what the French call 'le mot juste', not an easy thing when you are speaking a foreign language. Actually, it was more than a sense of 'the right word' – it was more a sense of 'the right thought', which made you feel that he had been able to articulate something mysterious, something you'd never have been able to pluck out of the ether yourself. Where most people would have rambled around the topic, groping for words, he was able to provide an effortless précis, and his aphorisms stuck in the mind. For example, he once said, 'Some people play long notes. Other people play short notes and hold them.' I would never have thought of putting it like that, but I saw at once what he meant. With that brilliant phrase he had given me a very useful tool for understanding the way that different musicians 'inhabit' the space of a note. When there was a roomful of musicians thinking about one of his 'aperçus', there was a lovely sense of 'entrainment', all of us carried on a little wave of insight.

His self-possession was remarkable. When he started to speak you felt confident that he had the whole thought in view and knew how he was going to structure it (so when I wrote down his sentences in my notebook, I didn't have to 'tidy them up' because they were perfectly formed). But that was not actually the most impressive thing: it was his ability, indeed his determination, to venture into psychological realms which any performer would recognise but which are not usually the subject of piano lessons. His teaching would probably not have been possible in any era before Freud and Jung had given us a vocabulary in which to talk about our behaviour, our feelings and their mysterious driving forces. Classical music and musicians, it seemed to me, was a perfect area to explore using that vocabulary, because the combination of art and human endeavour produced such a rich brew. The music was not easy to play and the instruments were not easy to handle. There was no end to the complexity of the results as people pitted themselves against great music they loved. In the course of that effort they sometimes had to come up against the limits of their imagination and their ability, but there was always the possibility that, with a bit of inspired guidance, they would discover they had more powers than they knew.

Sebök once said that he tried to 'open the channel' between his brain and his spinal cord so that information could flow upwards and downwards in a beneficial way. Can anyone really do that, I wondered? I tried to do it myself after he had described it, and although I may have been kidding myself, I felt there was something in it. Certainly it seemed to me that when Sebök paused, looked inscrutable and reached for a helpful sentence, he reached not into the standard vocabulary of music teachers but rather into the vocabulary of psychoanalysis, scientific principles, or indeed eastern mysticism. Had he not been a pianist and piano teacher he would probably have ended up writing a work of philosophy like David Hume's *Enquiry concerning Human Understanding*. For that is how his lessons struck me, and why I found them so memorable.

I am aware that some people feel that it is not necessary to put things into words. Many don't have the skill, or the wish to try, but of course it does *not* mean that they don't feel those things as keenly as the person who strives to verbalise them. Feeling things and being able to express them are two different things, and in some fields it is irrelevant whether you are good at explaining yourself or not. Many musicians seem to feel that it is, in fact, important *not* to put things into words because by doing so you spoil the freshness of the experience. Music is a thorny issue in this respect because it is so evidently beyond words or, at any rate, does not run on a straightforwardly parallel track to words. Why would it be helpful, then, to use words? I have plenty of friends and colleagues who almost despise the attempt to put things into words and would prefer not to mediate the experience of music. They feel music just as deeply. But they don't have a need to say anything about it, and this habit has reached such a pitch amongst professional musicians (at least in the UK) that a desire to speak about the music or the performance marks a person out as 'not one of us'. Trying to put into words how you felt about the music almost makes you suspect, as if it is evidence that feeling has been diverted into the dry channel of words rather than remaining where it should, in the realm of the unsayable. It is far more usual amongst musicians to go for a drink after a concert and speak about anything but the music.

The disinclination to speak about music and the performance of music is completely understandable, though it also means that your experience of music remains a private matter. This is no problem if you are a performer, but it is arguably a handicap if you are a teacher or educator. It can be disappointing for your students if you are unable or unwilling to try and say what you think is happening, or should be happening, and why. If you are a good musician, able to express through your playing exactly what you want and mean, then perhaps your students will understand you (a great demonstration is worth a thousand words). But of course not everyone can play exactly as they want or mean, and not every student can extract a lesson just from listening. People are receptive to different things – for example, I have friends who 'see' colours, shapes and textures when they listen to music, and others who find that words and thoughts come into their minds as they listen; perhaps it is a matter of how the neural pathways connect in an individual's brain, and what for each person constitutes a 'full palette' of sensory or linguistic information. I have had music teachers who tried to show me things by playing them for me, miming them for me, and by taking my shoulders and moving me about physically to show

147

me what 'inner waves' the music had, but I am a person who tends to associate music with thoughts and (eventually) words, and I find it incredibly touching when a person tries to speak about something transcendent like music. The fact that it's difficult to speak about music makes me value it the more when people succeed in doing it. I know that music and words are not equivalents. I understand that when you put something into words, there's a danger of 'fixing' it so that its essential ambiguity is spoiled. But that is not the only possible result from trying to put something into words. Over and over again, while teaching or giving lecture-recitals, I have found that if I can find some kind of parallel in words for a musical gesture, it can suddenly open up the music for people in a way that allows them to enter and form a relationship with something previously inaccessible. I even feel that words can be helpful in pointing out music's beautiful ambiguity.

Scientists tell us that music may have developed before speech in the evolution of human language. If this is so, then one might suppose that music would be closer to everyone's heart than words are, but one sees time and time again that many people find words easier to relate to. Words are our everyday currency and we know what they mean, even when they are used in a special way, such as in poetry or drama. By contrast, the language of music is more remote. Obviously some people 'get it' instinctively, but there are many people who enjoy having an avenue of words provided for them. I know this now for sure after being told so by lots of different people who have been to concerts or classes where I or a chamber music partner spoke about music. And I believe that the *spoken* word has a special quality. Although words are close to all of us, the written word retains an element of effort for many people, even if they like reading. The spoken word on the other hand just goes straight into our ears and minds, along with the tone of voice used by the speaker.

Every school child finds it completely normal to be asked to discuss or write 'comprehensions' about poetry, their response to it, and what the author does to create his or her effects. It is acknowledged that poetry provides a way to access elevated and mysterious feelings, or to put together facets of experience in an unusual, humorous or insightful way, and that it is good for young people – even those who are not enthusiasts – to have some understanding of how poems do what they do, even having a go at writing poems themselves. When a major poet like Alice Oswald says that 'poetry is what happens when language becomes impossible', her observation is taken seriously, and teachers are motivated to set out with their students to explore what she might mean. But the same is not generally true of music, which (at least in the schools I know) is considered a non-academic subject and, indeed, a 'participant sport' not in need of analysis. I went through my whole school career without ever being asked, or offered an explanation for, why music moved me. We did 'close reading' of literature almost every day, but never close reading of music, even though it is another prime example of what happens when language becomes impossible. Although discussing the effect of music is not on the curriculum, that does not mean there is no appetite for such discussion among music-lovers. The ability to speak about music is a valuable attribute in an educator – even if few educators have developed the art of speaking about music as Sebök had.

'What's missing from your playing is self-appreciation', he said one day to a Japanese girl who had just given a respectful performance of Ravel's 'Alborada del Gracioso'. 'You should be busy enough so that you love the music and have less time to criticise yourself. You say that you love the piece, but you love it all the time except when you play it. Maybe you love it in private, but you should know how to love it publicly. "Alborada" is the kind of piece for which witnesses are very important. If you shut the audience out of your mind and try to think of them as cabbages [he said smilingly], you must realise that cabbages don't think, but they also don't *love* you. The public just reflects you. They cannot dance or bounce unless you do.' In a minute of advice he had given material for years of constructive practising. Just his observation that she 'loved the music all the time except when she played it' was incredibly helpful to this onlooker at least. I did the same; when I performed, the sense of love changed into a sense of responsibility. Responsibility to my teacher, to my parents, to the composer, to the audience. All of them seemed to need something from me. What leisure was there in which to love the music?

I recalled his observation about cabbages years later when on behalf of a nervous student I tried to find out about seminars designed to help performers overcome stage fright. Nervous performers were often advised to visualise the audience in a way that made them seem unthreatening or even ridiculous. Imagining the audience sitting there in their underwear was one such tactic – the idea being that it would be hard to feel afraid of an audience so undignified. But why would you want to play to such an audience? An audience in its underwear, no matter how helpfully discomfited, would not be in a fit state to respond to you or the music either. I thought of Sebök's cabbages sitting there greenly in their rows. It seemed rather unfair to single out cabbages as an example of an inert audience. I found myself thinking that playing to an audience of cabbages *who loved me* would be a wholly delightful experience.

One day a girl complained that studying at the Juilliard School in New York was so competitive that it had ruined her enjoyment of music. Playing the piano now felt like a chore. 'It must handicap you a lot not to have fun', said Sebök. 'When a soldier walks ten miles, he is tired because he does it from duty. A tourist can walk ten miles and not be tired because he does it for fun. Love of duty is not an inspiring force, but love of music is. Give yourself permission to have fun. Don't accuse Juilliard, but don't dislike yourself either, because that leaves you with nothing. Your practice should not be done from a sense of duty, but because it is interesting. If it is not interesting, don't do it! Make yourself thirsty for music, and don't play until you are. Then you will love it, and you will feel how music tastes.'

'People who become very anxious before concerts are sometimes so because of a sense of responsibility', Sebök had said. 'But it is the responsibility of a child, who feels that he will be punished for getting things wrong, or, if he is not punished, will punish himself.' Here again was the psychoanalyst's consulting-room. I was struck by his astute addition of the phrase, 'or, if he is not punished, will punish himself'.

He didn't want his advice to be slavishly followed, however. 'You remembered everything I said, bar by bar, about that piece to the last person who played it', he said to a girl who had attended someone else's lesson on the same piece. 'But you didn't digest that information, because if you had, I wouldn't have remembered all my own comments as they surfaced one by one.' On another occasion he said, 'It is very interesting to discover that if you play *any way* but your usual way, it's much better!' Such advice didn't suit people who wanted to be told how to play. But for those of us who were looking for a way to avoid becoming stale with music we had studied a lot, it was liberating. 'For example,' said Sebök humorously, 'play standing up. And you can say to yourself that if you play in a strange way when you're standing up, your usual habits are prevented and something better is revealed. And that better thing is you.' This was unorthodox but intriguing advice.

'I hate artificial attitudes, artificial ecstasies', he once said. 'I hate seeing this ...' (he sat at the piano, miming the way that pianists close their eyes and seem to go into a trance at the beauty of the music) '... because it anticipates something that hasn't happened yet. This kind of artificial trance ... there is no reason for it; nothing happened yet! There is no reason to be ecstatic. No: the attitude comes from the music. I don't put my attitude on it. That music comes from Chopin's mind, not mine.' It seemed so obvious when he demonstrated the superfluousness of the 'trance', and yet the trance is encountered in performers everywhere. I had never been directly told to do it, and yet it was 'in the air' that closing your eyes and looking moved, even before you had played anything moving or felt moved anew by the music, was a traditional part of performing

151

(and not only in classical music). I resolved only to allow myself to look moved if something moving had just occurred. I do think that trying to get into a meditative state of mind can be useful, even necessary, but looking painfully moved in advance is probably one of the things that alienates listeners, and is best avoided.

When I first played to him, both in chamber music and on my own, I was not able to write down what he said as we went along, and it is a curious thing that my notes on my own lessons are very brief and plain. In truth, I was puzzled. We had so looked forward to hearing what Sebők had to say, what brilliant advice he would give us to make our goals clearer and our rehearsals more effective. In fact, as I remember, he told us that we were very good musicians and that we were spending too much time in 'digging around' and trying to find things to discuss and work on, rather than just enjoying the freshness of the musical experience. He told us that rehearsing all the time was not necessarily the way to achieve what we wanted. I was not sure what he was driving at. Why wasn't he analysing our foibles, diagnosing the gap between our dream and our reality? It was true that we were digging around, trying out and discussing a million different ways of doing things. We thought we were being conscientious musicians, rather than 'trying to find things to discuss and work on', which made it sound a bit pointless. Having expected to be told how to think to more purpose, I was taken aback to be told that I was thinking too much and should just get on with it. But what about everyone else in the class whom he was constantly telling to think more, feel more, think in a different way? They were getting such great advice. I wanted great advice too. It wasn't hugely helpful (I thought) to be told, in effect, that 'if it ain't broke, don't fix it'. It turned out that 'not over-thinking' was to be a running theme in my lessons with Sebők.

Sebők's advice was not only metaphysical. He was also very knowledgeable about anatomy, physiology and the musician's use of muscles. He had many helpful things to say about the pianist's posture and physical attitude. 'Keep the triangle of shoulder blades and the small of the back as compact as possible', he advised, 'and keep the stomach relaxed.' He mentioned that the pianist has three points of contact with the rest of the world: the feet on the floor, the bottom on the chair, and the hands on the keyboard. Any of these three points are in danger of becoming tense, and if they do then there are consequences in the pianist's sound and the way they can communicate music. He advised us to think of these three points as being 'open'. He pointed out that many pianists lean forwards and 'nail down' the solar plexus, which we should try not to do. If they lean forward, then straightaway at least one of the 'three points' will become tense.

Leaning forward was a very common problem; 'many pianists abase themselves in front of the piano', he said shrewdly. Almost as many pianists lean back, which makes their task more difficult, because leaning back is actually quite strenuous, especially for the abdominal muscles, and like leaning forward, it results in the solar plexus being unavailable for proper breathing. He observed that neither leaning forward nor leaning back is physically helpful, yet the pianist who sits upright in a relaxed fashion is a rare sight. It was true, but there was a reason for it, which of course he knew: almost all of us had 'posture issues' because we weren't just sportspeople – we were emotionally engaged with the task of making music through playing the instrument. Why did we lean forward or lean back when it would have made our lives easier not to? That was a big question which clearly had a psychological dimension. It was very helpful to have one's attention drawn to it, because from time to time it was possible to catch oneself in the act of leaning forward or back for no good reason, and it felt good to regain one's balance.

One of Sebök's most important observations was that pianists are often too influenced by the fact that they play the piano sitting down. 'Their wave of movement goes from their head to the piano stool and stops. But there should be a longer wave which goes right down to the ground.' I experimented with this and it felt good. If I visualised a whole wave from my head to the floor, it helped me to have an upright posture. Sometimes the upright posture is denigrated by onlookers because it makes the pianist appear 'disengaged', but actually it is the most helpful position from which to mobilise the hands and arms.

'When playing a loud staccato chord,' he told a student, 'don't let the diaphragm tighten because then the chord will have a kind of recoil [he used the German word 'Nachklang']. And don't play as if the keyboard were terribly hot! Relax the stomach, drop the forearm like a hammer. Prepare for as long as you need to lift the arm – like preparing to throw a stone – but when you have thrown the stone, let it go. Neutralisation of the body before a loud dry chord is very important, like before you hit something with a hammer. Don't lean back as a form of preparation.' The student tried to do what he'd said. 'And don't use blind courage, hitting without wanting to *hear* the result', Sebök said. 'Have provocative courage. Prepare the chord and let it *land,* knowing what sound you will hear.' (That term 'provocative courage' was a wonderful instance of his choice of words.) That was very illuminating for me because blind courage was certainly one of my methods. Yet after he mentioned it, it wasn't so very difficult to add the element of 'knowing what sound you will hear', which made all the difference.

'If you know how to get access to your body, you will gain better access to your mind', he told another student. 'If you know yourself, you'll know which parts of the body are usually tense; with most people it's the tight neck, and of course the breathing. Imagine yourself as three pyramids, from feet to pelvis, bottom of the spine to shoulders, neck to head. Be in an unstable balance and accept the risks thereof.'

'Think of inner space', he told us. 'Think of the expanding universe, a beautiful image. In an expanding universe, every point moves away from every other point. Imagine two points at the top and bottom of your spine. Imagine those points moving away from one another – not just the top one getting higher, or the bottom one getting lower, but both at once. Feel the inner space that results!

Feel the difference in the sound.'

When I came back from Canada, I started attending his summer courses in the Swiss village of Ernen, in the German-speaking part of the Valais. His Ernen course had a rather different atmosphere from that of Banff because while in Banff he was one of a whole roster of visiting professors, in Ernen the whole course revolved around him. The reputation of the course had spread far and wide, and the intake was international, with many Japanese and American participants. We all had to figure out how to get to Switzerland and then by increasingly rural train lines to the village of Ernen, which lay in the mountains among flower-filled meadows. Students rented little chalets around the village, and there were other chalets in which hired upright pianos had been put so that we could practise. When I had finished practising it was my pastime to go out in the meadows to pick the astonishingly colourful Alpine flowers to make the chalet look homely. Once or twice a day we all gathered together in the large school room where Sebök taught.

In these lessons he continued to speak about the importance of freedom and the way that we can become prisoners of our habits. Just as he had once advised us to try playing 'any other way' than the way we usually played, he reminded us that while daily practice is necessary to keep one's hands and fingers agile, it also tends to encourage the sheer repetition which ends up becoming mindless playing (in fact, the kind of 'semi-automatic function' which he had warned us about in Canada). A girl in the class, who had studied for a long time with Sebök in America, once told me that she hated seeing him on concert days because when she was trying to achieve a polished performance, she needed to 'fix' certain things in her mind and found it unsettling to be reminded that it might be fruitful to try it in a different way, no matter how true that might be. Even if he didn't say anything on a concert day, she said she could feel him looking at her with his bright appraising glance and thinking something like, 'Another person who is a prisoner of her habits.' She and I agreed that most of us cannot afford to leave everything open until the moment of performance. Quite apart from what we do with the music itself, there are many other ingredients of the performance situation (nerves, self-consciousness) which make it helpful to decide and practise in advance exactly what you're going to do. Intellectually we could see that leaving things open to the spur of the moment might be exciting, but what if there wasn't any spur of the moment? For the sake of our peace of mind we all practised towards a clearly-imagined result. We felt downhearted when Sebök said things like, 'Some of your gestures mean freedom. Others mean slavery.'

And yet his talk of freedom was judicious; he didn't think that being open to other ways of doing things was a universal panacea. He once memorably said that one could be a slave to the idea of freedom. 'As a teacher,' he once said to a student who was 'expressing himself' through the Liszt sonata, 'although I'm always talking about freedom, there comes a moment when things are no longer relative, because I have to believe in *something*. I can hear people play things in all kinds of different versions and I can say yes, this can be right; and this; and this too; but not *that*. **That** is wrong. You don't have the freedom not to respect the composer's wishes. If he writes "piano", you are not free to play "forte". When I hear you play, I feel that you are not looking for this sonata; you're looking for something in yourself.'

How many times since then have I felt like using that same sentence when I've been teaching other people! 'You're not looking for this piece – you're looking for something in yourself.' In fact it sometimes feels as if this 'looking for yourself, expressing yourself' is the main field of interest for many people, and they might even be backed up by contemporary theorists who believe that the music is there to give the player something to play, not the other way round. In other words, the player's experience is all-important, especially if the composer is dead. But Sebök was not a fan of such thinking. I was almost relieved that there was something about which he was not prepared to be flexible. Well, perhaps 'relieved' is not the correct way of describing my feelings, for after all I had had years of listening to teachers not being flexible, and I was thrilled to find someone who was genuinely not attached to a particular way of doing things, but I enjoyed it when the kaleidoscope of ideas came to an occasional halt in front of certain facts. He believed that it was the composer who inspired the player, not the player who bestowed their inspiration on the composer. One of his sayings was, 'Don't resonate. Don't identify. *Understand.*' This seems to me the only beneficial way to look at it if you are in music for the long haul, because if your own feelings are the measure of your art, they may prove to be limited in comparison to the thoughts and feelings of the person who wrote the music and relied on you to communicate it. Perhaps this is not so with every kind of music, but it must be true of great music, which renews itself for every generation.

Sebök once said that understanding was 'not an intellectual thing' but rather a way of 'being with' the music in full sympathy and appreciation. Even though I was sure he was right about that, it was sometimes hard to know how to alter one's way of practising accordingly, because in the long hours you spend getting to know and mastering a difficult piece of music, you can't proceed only on instinct. At least, I couldn't. I had my instinctive musical response to the piece, but in parallel with that I developed a sort of meta-narrative of thoughts and knowledge about it. Sebök said that knowing that a piece was in A flat major was of no consequence when responding to it, but I found that such knowledge could actually help to inform one's understanding – for example by being able to compare it to other works in the same key, to think about the particular character of that key and why the composer had chosen it rather than another. The key of A flat has a certain 'feel' under the hands, and that adds its own flavour to one's understanding. There were lots of similar examples. You could say that it was 'intellectual' to know how the piece was structured, for example, but the structure is a very important part of how the piece communicates. Sebök knew this, of course, but he still thought there was a way of forgetting all such information and learning how to 'be in the moment' with the music, so that you as a musician were as pleased and surprised as everyone else by the way it unfolded, even though you had practised it a trillion times. The paradox was that it was almost impossible to reach this state of 'oneness with the music' unless you *had* practised it a trillion times, and if you had then you would find it vanishingly hard to retain your sense of what was surprising about it. To set out to be surprised by something you knew was coming felt like an impossible task. Yet we knew there was something profound in it. When you listen to the best performances they do not strike you as 'old news'. They seem freshly created in the moment.

In the class in Ernen there was an American man, Glenn, who was there every summer as a listener. I think he had first gone along out of casual interest to support a girlfriend who wanted to play to Sebök, and was so captivated that he returned on his own year after year. Glenn didn't play a musical instrument, but he was intensely musical, sensitive and empathetic, and got endless joy out of Sebök's ability to put his finger on important things in lessons. Glenn was also interested in Zen Buddhism and he told me that the crux of his interest in the piano classes was that one so often saw people confronting the paradox of how to make the music come alive despite having worked on it for so long. He agreed with Sebök that although it was a good thing to enquire into all kinds of aspects of the music, its history, its structure, its performance tradition and so on, it was important to know when to stop doing that and let all that information sink down to a subconscious layer.

Some people didn't have to fight to do this because they didn't spend all that much time acquiring knowledge of the music beyond the notes. Others, like me and my colleagues, found it very hard to be the musician who knows what is coming and yet also the musician who can still respond to what is coming as it comes. Sebök once accused me of sounding as if I was 'reciting an emotion I had learned by heart' when I played a sad movement of Beethoven. I *had* learned the emotion by heart and didn't see how I could have done otherwise. It was my aim to understand the sad emotion and communicate it to the audience. I had thought about what kind of sadness it was and what kind of tone to use to express it. So I was frustrated when he said it didn't sound as if I was sad *now*. Actually what he was asking for is one of the hardest things to achieve in performance, and few people achieve it. I knew what he meant and I could see it was the right thing to aim for – I just didn't know how to do it without aiming for it. Glenn said that it was like that famous Zen riddle which asks, 'You meet the master unexpectedly. Do not salute him, do not ignore him. What do you do?'

One very helpful piece of advice was when Sebök said, 'Don't play from the shoulders; find a longer wave and play from the bottom of the back. Energy comes from somewhere in the body, and if, as a metaphor, you imagine the energy coming from a low point in the body, you'll lift your arm from somewhere low too. You will play with the whole person, and even one note will sound important if the whole person plays.' Was this Zen, or poetry?

Glenn played an unwitting part in a strange experience I had when I played to Sebök in Ernen. I was playing Beethoven's Sonata in A flat opus 110, a hugely difficult piece I had been practising for months with this moment in mind (and Sebök would probably have said that that was part of the problem). Mine was the first lesson of the afternoon session and I was able to practise the piano in the lesson room while it was empty during the lunch break. I was sitting at the piano, feeling very nervous and keyed-up as all the listeners filed back in from lunch and took their places. Sebök came over to me and whispered, 'It's Glenn's birthday today. Before you begin, could you play "Happy Birthday" for him, as a surprise? We can all sing.'

Talk about being de-railed! I was thoroughly 'thrown', but I didn't want to refuse a request from Sebök, who had never before asked me to do anything for him. It came into my head that I had recently heard someone give a very amusing rendition of 'Happy Birthday' on the piano, starting with the magnificent opening bars of Tchaikovsky's first piano concerto and then, instead of bringing in Tchaikovsky's grand orchestral theme, bringing in the tune of Happy Birthday. The juxtaposition of Tchaikovsky's first piano concerto and Happy Birthday had caused a great deal of hilarity and I thought it would be fun to make people laugh in the same way. I pushed Beethoven out of my mind and raised my hands to play the opening of the Tchaikovsky piano concerto. But as soon as I tried to put my hands on the keys, a weird thing happened: I got the most violent 'pins and needles' in my hands, so violent that I could hardly play a note. It was as if an electrical storm had broken out in my forearms. Never before had I experienced something like that (and never again have I experienced it, 'touch wood'). It felt as though I were having a panic attack, except that the symptoms were confined to my arms and hands. I somehow managed to stagger through the Tchaikovsky/Happy Birthday mash-up (with everyone singing) and then, when the laughter had died down, I prepared to play my Beethoven. But my hands were still trembling violently, and the 'pins and needles' were painful. I had no idea what was happening to me. I could only think that Sebök's unexpected diversion had caused some kind of minor apoplexy – that's certainly what it felt like. With greater presence of mind I might have asked if I could have a moment to go out of the room to take a few deep breaths and recover, but I had no presence of mind at that moment (it was probably my only real experience of debilitating platform nerves). Unwisely I launched into my Beethoven, a piece I had played hundreds of times without physical strain but which now felt like a bucking horse that had to be controlled by sheer will-power. Or rather, my hands felt as if they belonged to someone else and had to be wrestled into my control. I was on the verge of tears, which I later discovered had made my performance seem rather moving, except to those who knew me well enough to realise that something was amiss.

Much later, I of course wondered whether Sebök, knowing my tendency to 'over-think', had deliberately tried to intervene in my thinking process and put me in an unexpected position by springing on me the request to play Happy Birthday. Very likely it was not an intervention at all. He probably just had a sudden notion, and didn't consider its effect on me. But he was sitting at a second grand piano beside mine – he could have played Happy Birthday to Glenn himself. I could only think that he felt it would be funny for everyone to hear me playing Happy Birthday instead of the late Beethoven sonata which was on the programme. I was exasperated with him, though when I finished the Beethoven sonata I couldn't help noticing the roar of applause which greeted the final bar of my performance. Afterwards it was interesting to hear people say that my playing had seemed 'very personal'. One of my old friends said he 'could hear the turbulent emotions of my private life coming through clearly in the music for the first time'. Normally, he said, I tried to leave those turbulent emotions behind when I performed. This was true. To me the performance space was a special place where I could transcend my personal problems.

By temperament and by 'ethical choice' I agreed with Sebök when he had said that we musicians need to be very careful of what we are making the audience understand. 'Imagine a man who is intrigued by the character of Napoleon', he said. 'This man reads the famous biography of Napoleon written by Emil Ludwig [in 1915]. After this he feels that he knows Napoleon personally. He is so struck by Ludwig's insight into Napoleon that he decides to read a biography of Ludwig. He does so. Gradually he understands why Ludwig, because of his own experiences, interpreted Napoleon's life as he did. In the process, the reader starts to understand Ludwig more, and loses his sense of knowing Napoleon.'

'In the same way,' Sebök continued, 'if you become fascinated by Casals' playing of Bach, you think it is Bach you understand. Then you study the life of Casals ... and so on.'

His warning made sense to me. It was not my aim to make people understand more and more about me. On the contrary, it was my wish to 'disappear' as much as possible on stage so that the listeners would have an unmediated experience of the music. I don't mean that I wanted to be self-effacing on stage (in fact I hoped to be appreciated), but rather that I would try to leave my personal problems behind when I played to other people. Naturally no performer can prevent the audience from noticing things and having thoughts about them when they are on stage, but they can certainly try not to make themselves, as opposed to the music, the centre of attention. This was my aim. I was disconcerted when people said they were touched by seeing me struggling not to weep in my Beethoven lesson. For the truth was that I wasn't especially moved by the *music* that afternoon; I was struggling because my hands felt as if they had been plugged into the National Grid. If I was moved, it was by my own plight. The fact that the audience warmed to me because of it didn't fit with my 'purist' ethos. As for being especially moved by the music, I'd guess that I was *more* engaged with it in my practice studio when my hands and my nervous system were behaving normally. In any case, no matter how excited the listeners may have been by the sight of me struggling, it was obvious that this was not a scenario that could be 'manufactured' in the future. I couldn't *pretend* to be struggling in order to arouse people's sympathy.

Sebök had once spoken about the Swiss pianist Clara Haskil and how she could 'disappear' when playing. It seemed an admirable thing, her ego-less ability to convey Mozart as purely as possible without trying to serve up Clara Haskil alongside. Sebök drew a comparison with one of the windows in the classroom. 'That window disappears when I look through it at the mountains beyond', he said. 'And yet I do not respect it for disappearing. Its purpose is to disappear. When a performer manages to disappear, we know how difficult it is for a human being to do that. If I listen to Clara Haskil and feel that I hear not Clara Haskil but Mozart, then it is a sign of the highest artistry.'

When we speak of a classical performer 'disappearing' in an 'ego-less' manner, that is a kind of poetic licence, because even a pianist like Clara Haskil did not want to disappear so completely that we did not notice it was her. In fact, like every other pianist she hoped to make – and did make – a career based on her particular skills and the special aura of her performances. No pianist wants to disappear to the extent that the public thinks any other pianist would do just as well. It was Haskil's aim, I feel sure, to convey Mozart as 'purely' as possible but, unlike the window through which we admire the distant mountains, I suppose she *did* want to be respected. The tradition, perhaps to be found in most classical art forms, of 'disappearing' or remaining anonymous is something quite delicate, prone to paradox. Yes, the performer wants you to hear Mozart and nothing but Mozart, but they also depend on your noticing that they, *in particular*, are able to bring about that feeling that they have selflessly stood aside for the greater glory of the person whose music they are playing, or the glory of the music itself. To be a classical performer in that tradition is a curious blend of appearing and disappearing, and depends on an audience which understands that subtle tension.

In London I once or twice went to play to Peter Feuchtwanger, who was a great admirer of Clara Haskil and had purchased some of her concert dresses as souvenirs. Already then they seemed to speak of a bygone approach to a concert career. They were long, black, severe, high-necked, long-sleeved, a little forbidding. They flaunted no part of the body. One outfit was a plain white shirt worn with a heavy black jacket and long stiff skirt (as one can see in the photographs of her with violinist Arthur Grumiaux). In their heavy, high-quality plain fabrics her outfits emanated respect for tradition and the status of the classical pianist, plus a strong disinclination for vulgar self-display. In the time since those lessons, it seems to me that performers' goals have changed. There are still artists whose aim is to 'disappear' in a benevolent way, and there probably always will be. But now there is much more emphasis on the visual aspects of performance, and even more impactfully, on the 'celebrity' qualities and the lifestyle of the performer. It is noticeable in every musical genre. The personal life, the clothes sense, the hairstyle, the platform behaviour – all have gained an importance parallel to, or even greater than, the musicianship. Magazine articles about celebrity musicians are not principally about the music or their approach to it, but rather about peripheral things (partly because it is much easier to write about peripheral things). Struggles with mental health problems or family feuds are not only not hidden, but are accepted and even promoted as legitimate communication tools.

As far as I remember, the whole subject of platform manner and dress meant nothing to Sebök except in so far as it had a bearing on the way the music was communicated. I never heard him speak about how to get on or off the stage, what to wear, or how to endear yourself to the audience. He was allergic to any kind of 'pantomime' drawing attention to the performer. I remember him once mimicking a boy who had played some Liszt in a way that Sebök found vulgar, for example playing loud chords with his right hand and then continuing the movement of his hand down past the keyboard and towards the floor, letting his arm swing back and forth from the shoulder theatrically. Sebök looked at him with dislike, and without saying a word, turned to the piano and played the same passage, imitating what the student had just done and letting his own right arm swing theatrically. It looked ridiculous and the young man flushed with displeasure as he realised he was being imitated.

Yet to that same student he went on to give some great advice. 'The sound effects and textures in Liszt must be the right scale', he explained. 'If I hope to hear the image of a butterfly, but instead I receive the image of a Boeing 747, it's out of scale. You must realise that when Liszt writes these waves of sound, that really enormous waves travel deeply and slowly. They give the feeling of more *beneath* than on top.' This was advice that he could work with straightaway, and he did. The waves of sound became more than mere virtuosic display, and we could begin to imagine why Liszt's playing caused such a sensation in his day. Liszt was a composer Sebök was particularly fond of, and he often said that Liszt's imagination as a composer was not properly appreciated. He was frustrated that Liszt's piano music was known primarily for its pyrotechnics. 'Liszt is often used like the potato was used when first imported into Europe: people didn't know how to treat it, so they ate the leaves and threw away the potato', he told us. I had never 'rated' Liszt, but Sebök's demonstrations of Liszt were something we looked forward to. I found it very helpful when he commented that 'for Liszt, it didn't matter whether a passage was in octaves or not in octaves. For him, octaves were a matter of orchestration, not a doubling of physical effort.' He played a wildly difficult passage to show us what he meant. At the end he looked round with a twinkling smile and said, 'When I play that passage, I don't feel as if I'm fighting; I feel as if I'm succeeding.'

On the subject of physical effort, he had helpful things to say about breathing. 'The lungs must work freely ... If we get away from breathing, then we die', he had told *Piano Quarterly*. 'Breath is not related exactly to musical phrases or tempo, but it is related to our actual living. When doing something very complicated which involves focused mental states, one has to go on and breathe freely. Concentration usually slows down breath; physical activity speeds it up. If I play the finale of the Tchaikovsky concerto, then I have to breathe faster because I am doing something physically demanding and at the same time I am compelled to breathe less because I am concentrating too much. That's a contradiction. One has to find a way to go on breathing freely in spite of the mental effort, and be able to breathe faster if the physical effort demands it.' That is a very good analysis of the breathing problem, though as any performer will tell you, 'breathing freely in spite of the mental effort' is one of the hardest things to achieve. For example, I find that when I am concentrating, I hold my breath. I sometimes come off stage and take gulps of air as I become conscious that I haven't been breathing properly. From anecdotal evidence, I think that many performers find the same. Yet nobody had ever addressed this problem in piano lessons. I found that after having my attention drawn to it, I was at least able to stage the occasional intervention in my own physical habits and set myself breathing again. He was right: if we are not breathing, we are not free to react to things around us.

How breathing relates to phrasing in music is an enormous topic. It came up in my lesson on Beethoven when we started to look at various points in the music where, as often happens in Beethoven's 'late' pieces, he switches suddenly and without warning from one mood to another. Characteristically, it gives a powerful sense of 'I haven't got time to explain this to you', or even 'I'm not going to explain this.' In his earlier music there are dramatic changes of mood, often 'signalled' to the listener by means of some kind of transition or 'winding-down' or winding-up' which makes the change of mood more understandable when it comes. In his late music he often omits the transitions and simply flips from one mood or character to another, sometimes from one beat to the next. There are several examples in the A flat sonata we were studying. There are also many places where Beethoven requires the player to go from 'forte' to 'piano' or the other way round in a split second. The question was whether to help everyone make sense of what was happening by using *timing*. A big change of mood, or a lightning switch from loud to soft, often takes the performer a moment or two to 'feel' in their own body. (As Sebök said, 'The continuation has to start in your body, not only in your mind.') Sometimes a new muscle group is needed to produce sudden loud sound, or sudden whispering sound. It can't be done absolutely instantly, or at least, if it is done instantly, it does not seem lifelike. Instead it often seems, even to the performer, as if the psychological link between the two things has been sucked out by the speed of the change. Is that what Beethoven wanted? We can't know, but we pianists can know what it is like to *perform* the music to an audience, and possibly that is a situation he never experienced. By the time of his late music, his deafness meant that he no longer played concerts.

A change from fast motion to slow, or slow to fast, from a peaceful character to an angry one or vice versa, is not easy to bring alive in performance unless you use the dimension of time to create a sort of space in which the listener's understanding can catch up. When you have the chance to practise something for months and months, your own understanding has already caught up. I had found in practice sessions that with some concentrated effort (and probably without breathing) I could 'turn on a dime' and flip from one character to another or from one dynamic to another without needing any 'rubato' to achieve it. But when I unveiled my trick of going suddenly from loud to soft, Sebök smiled and told me that it 'didn't sound like a *subito piano*, but like someone suddenly turning the radio down'. [He leaned over and mimed turning my volume control down, and everyone laughed.] 'Some human logic is missing', he said, '... the co-operation of *time* with *action*.' The listener, he said, would not have had my opportunity to get used to it all. If I turned on a dime, listeners might be left behind. The change of character might be incomprehensible to them; the suddenness of the change might seem heartless. They might lose the thread and never catch up (this is, I gradually discovered, a danger with performances of late Beethoven).

The discussion made me attentive to what other performers do when they play late Beethoven. It can certainly be baffling if they negotiate the violent mood changes as though there were no effort involved in doing so. On the page there is no effort. But the performer may sense the effort when they try to 'activate' the music. They cannot help having physiological reactions when they play, especially if they are properly engaged with the music. If they suppress their physical reactions, they may seem robotic rather than convincing. There seemed to be some ideal balance whereby at moments of sudden change in the music, the player could – by allowing themselves to have a natural reaction – create a 'human scale' of timing. On the other hand they were not to be self-indulgent, milking the moment for theatre when perhaps neither the composer nor the audience would want or need this. Sebök constantly reminded us that it is egotistical to put your own construction on something whose construction is already of a larger stature. His attitude is perhaps 'old-fashioned' today when theorists in fields such as literary criticism tell

167

us that the published book is no longer the author's but the reader's, and that whatever the reader thinks it means is what it means. This was not a view Sebök would have endorsed.

Being faithful to the composer's wishes remains a difficult interpretative problem because although Beethoven sometimes uses very complicated notation to write exactly what he wants, there are many things that he doesn't notate at all. If you study what Beethoven did notate and what he didn't notate, it is not clear why some things (for example, permission to pause or take time at certain moments) are not notated. It could be that conventional notation just doesn't offer ways to notate what is essentially a 'live transaction' between the player and the audience. Or it could be that Beethoven simply assumed that any intelligent pianist would do something appropriate by instinct.

Perhaps the performer may actually know more about the ingredients of mood swings than the composer did. After all, the composer may never have actually tried playing the piece to an audience, and making the piece come alive involves various elements, never notated, which are left to the performer to discover and negotiate. I was reminded of this recently when the poet-performer Kate Tempest said in a *Guardian* interview that, as a writer, she knew a certain amount about her own text, but when she performed it for an audience, 'Kate the performer learned more about it than Kate the writer ever dreamed of'. If any remark could encapsulate why performance studies are important, hers can.

Sebök told me that when he listened to me playing my Beethoven sonata he could 'hear me talking to myself about my comprehension of the piece'. He said he was aware of me asking myself, 'What shall I do?', instead of dropping my intellectual thoughts down to a deeper level and simply allowing myself to be in the music as a fish is in water. Naturally it was my most earnest wish to swim happily in the music like a fish, and I was exasperated that he perceived me as overlaying the music with my thoughts about what to do with it. My struggle to understand what he meant became even more complicated when he observed that all my thoughts were good ones, important ones, thoughts that he didn't often hear people engaging with, but all the same he didn't want to be aware of them when he was listening to me play. He said that when I was playing chamber music, where I seemed to feel absolutely at home, he always felt comfortable listening to me and felt that I was able to take care of the composer's well-being and enjoy the activity of music-making without being overly aware of what I was doing. When I played solo piano music, I became a degree more self-conscious and along with that seemed to come a tendency to over-concentrate. He thought I did it out of a sense of responsibility, which in a way was something laudable, but not if the sense of responsibility persisted all the way into the performance itself.

'I just want to make sure I have tried to understand', I said feebly. 'I know you do', he said. 'But maybe you are like an over-conscientious gardener, who wants to make sure that his plants are growing properly, and in order to find out, he pulls them up by the roots to examine them by daylight. Of course, if a gardener pulls up his plants by the roots, he will kill them. He should leave them in the ground, because the plants will know what to do in the darkness. A gardener has to have trust.' I had heard him use a gardening metaphor before, in a lesson where Masako, a Japanese girl, had played him a Bach sarabande. 'You play the sarabande with extreme politeness towards each note,' he said to her, 'carefully tending it like a gardener and not wanting any note to become any other note. But one note does become another note and that is what makes music.' It was a striking metaphor. Because of Masako's body language it was easy to see her as a gardener respectfully tending each note, and easy to see the limitations of such an approach. But now a gardening metaphor was being used on me. I was aghast to be told that I was pulling the plant up by the roots in order to examine it. True enough, in my months of preparation I had tried to enquire into every little corner of the piece, because there is so much in it that doesn't just 'play itself'. I didn't think it was enough just to play what I saw in front of me, because that would have felt like the equivalent of 'hitting blindly'. It was a piece that seemed to call for emotional engagement as well as intellectual understanding, and I wouldn't have dreamed of turning up at Sebök's masterclass without having prepared it assiduously. This was the first time I had performed it in public. I mumbled something about having had to pluck up my courage in order to perform it in front of the class.

He looked at me shrewdly. 'You have courage', he said. 'But better would be to have trust.'

I knew that he had hit the nail on the head, but I wasn't sure that I knew what to do about it. As he had reminded me, understanding was not an intellectual thing. He often spoke to us about the ideal state of mind for a performer, 'dropping thoughts down to an unconscious level', 'pushing our concentration all the way out', trying to prevent ourselves from over-focusing by looking away from the music, away from the instrument. Even playing from memory should, he said, be a natural thing. 'Don't treat memorising as an unusual skill', he said. 'Remembering is normal. If something makes sense, it is easily remembered.' He said that if the work of preparation had been done, we could just 'forget it' when we came to the performance and let our innate musicianship take over. 'You don't need to rehearse', he had once said to me and Krysia Osostowicz when we were playing a duo sonata to him. 'You should know how to catch the butterfly with the powder still on its wings.'

That is also a Zen concept, and seems to surface in many different fields when students get to a really high level and want to advance still higher. A famous description of 'catching the butterfly' is Eugen Herrigel's *Zen in the Art of Archery*, where he describes his struggles to understand his teacher's insistence that 'he' should not loose the bow from the arrow, but that 'it' should. What was the 'it', and was it under the control of the 'he', or was it something else? Herrigel struggled mightily for a long while to understand it intellectually, but eventually concluded that it was not to be understood in that way. He tried to bring about the sensation of 'it' shooting in various different ways including tricking himself into not noticing what his bow arm was doing, or deliberately making his bow arm so tired that his muscles would eventually give way and let the arrow go without his conscious decision. All these attempts angered his teacher. Herrigel did eventually experience 'it' shooting, but as you would expect, it was not something he could put into words. It seemed to boil down to a sense of not being separate from the target, but being identified with it, so that ultimately there was nothing and no one that made the shot, and nothing that was shot at.

The paradox of trying to hold on to such a state of mind in performance is that if you think about trying to achieve it, you have already missed the point. This was my problem, and I daresay many other people's problem as well. When I was performing, I was sometimes able just to hear the music arise in a relaxed way, as though it had its own life, but the sensation came and went. Sometimes I was conscious of following the music with my mind, checking up on it phrase by phrase and steering it along the route I had devised for it. Occasionally I succeeded in 'pushing my concentration all the way out' as Sebök recommended. But let's face it: it is a difficult matter to do that in classical music where there is usually a lot going on, and an awful lot of notes to get right. We have all come across performers who play the notes without thinking about them, and that can be a very disappointing experience for the listener. It's very common to see musicians playing on auto-pilot, repeating actions they have done hundreds of times in the practice room and are merely reprising once again on stage. They are not thinking, but they may not be channelling the music either. Clearly, 'not thinking' was not the right recipe, and that was not what Sebök meant. Rather, it was, as he had told me, a matter of having trust, which is not easy to practise. It's a state of mind or attitude bound up with your personal life, your interaction with other people and how those events have affected you. I sensed that it was not really possible to 'try to have trust', because trying would get in the way of having it. One had to stop trying and just have it. 'You need fearlessness, not courage',

Sebök had said. 'Don't overcome your fear: get rid of it!'

I had some experience of 'overcoming fear' but not much idea of how to 'get rid of it'. I realised it wasn't much to do with my musical prowess; it was something larger, to do with my temperament and nervous system, and probably with my life experience. For me, the key seemed to be to discover how to be 'in the moment', able to rely on one's store of musical knowledge yet free to interact with the moment so that the music was not consciously steered but simply released into its natural element of time. As Sebök once observed beautifully, 'We have to know the piano's element as a fish knows the water, not as a hydraulic engineer knows the water.' For me, this 'fish in water' state of mind has been easier to achieve in chamber music where somehow the added ingredients of other people playing and doing interesting things seem to use up part of my concentration in a beneficial way, leaving just the right amount for my own playing. (I realise that not everyone feels this way about playing chamber music. Some pianists feel very uncomfortable with the 'added ingredients' of other musicians taking part in the performance.) Sebök once told me that when I played chamber music he could feel that there was room in my mind not only for the other musicians, but also for extraneous thoughts not to do with the music. This, he said, was curiously reassuring. He recommended me to allow myself, when I played on my own, to go on thinking about whatever it was that I thought about when I shared the music-making with others. I was bemused by this advice at first, but as time went by I found it liberating.

If one reads about high-level achievement in any field, one hears reflections of similar kinds from the makers, artists, sportspeople involved. 'The right amount of concentration and not more' is something that many people struggle with. Often they tell how they tried and tried and couldn't quite reach their goal, until one day something or other stopped them trying so hard and they found the way to do it, more or less by accident. Now, this is an impossible thing to write a recipe for, because I would guess you cannot reach such a state if you have not first put in the work. You may have 'beginners' luck' without putting in the work, but it won't last. It seems to be necessary first to grapple with all the elements that make up a high level of attainment in your chosen field and then to find a way of 'letting go' so that you are released to do your best.

I think it probably comes down to the right balance between work and play. We forget that in many languages the word for making music on an instrument is 'play' (French 'jouer', German 'spielen'). Mastering an instrument is a long road, especially for classical musicians, and it is easy to lose sight of the basic meaning of the word 'play', which conveys fun, freedom, experiment. 'Playing' the piano becomes synonymous with 'practising' the piano for many. Lots of people have told me over the years that piano lessons were never fun for them, and that is why they gave up playing the piano at the earliest opportunity. Of course this is a terrible shame, because music is very special, and should always be a pleasure. Naturally when playing becomes bound up with daily practice and earning a living, the feeling of 'play' is often very far from one's thoughts, but it is vital to keep in touch with it. It is a wonderful thing to be a conscientious musician, but one should still know how to have fun. This is not a trivial thing; 'fun' is shorthand for pleasure, joy and playfulness, some of life's best qualities and certainly ones which should not be remote from the musician's experience of making music.

Sebök himself often seemed to be having fun, especially when it came to demonstrating things in lessons. I've written elsewhere (for example in *Beyond the Notes*) about the brilliance of his demonstrations. Here we really saw the benefits of not being attached to one particular way of doing things, because he seemed to be free to use any passage of music to show whatever he liked. He could use his powers of observation to show someone how their chosen piece might sound if they could bypass their usual habits (which he could imitate). He had a marvellous grasp of how to make the music make sense. When he demonstrated it, we all felt the sense of it. Yet he never seemed so lost in the music that he didn't retain an almost humorous objectivity about the act of performing. I remember that he once said, 'Don't *feel* so much. *Do* more, and you will be surprised at the result.'

Curiously enough his objectivity was an ingredient in some of his most touching playing. This paradox was beautifully described by the American pianist Jeremy Denk in a *New Yorker* article of 8 April 2013. His act of recollection and tribute is a superb piece of writing, and many of his descriptions are Sebökian in their felicity. Denk writes about hearing Sebök play a concert in Oberlin, Ohio, which ended with Bach's B flat major partita and its final skipping gigue. At the end of it, 'the piece resolves, and the left hand leaps up several octaves, like a slingshot or a skipping stone ... While performing this devilish sleight of hand, Sebök appeared angelic and unperturbed. The words "musical" and "unmusical" did not apply. It was as if the concepts behind the notes, playful and profound, had come alive. As he revealed each audacious but logical chord change, I experienced both shock and comprehension – surprise at something that made perfect sense.'

I was touched by Denk's pair of words 'playful and profound'. I didn't hear that particular concert, but I knew just what he meant because I had had the same feeling umpteen times when listening to demonstrations in class. It looked ever so simple, but it was the kind of simplicity that comes after all the knots have been untied. Sebök had constantly told us that when we discover how to do something, we should stop asking ourselves questions. 'Take the attitude of someone doing something easy', he advised. 'Remember the aim is to *know* more, not to concentrate more. When you know more, you concentrate less.' I once heard him say to a Japanese student, 'I have the feeling that either you like effort, or you don't mind it. I *hate* effort. If I have to use effort, I feel I have not succeeded.' He himself seemed to have discovered the secret of playing from a wellspring of knowledge, but without undue concentration. We all watched and thought, 'That's what I must do.' As I wrote this sentence many years later, I was about to add '... but it wasn't so easy', when I suddenly imagined that if Sebök was looking over my shoulder at what I was writing, he might tap me on the shoulder, give me a glittering look and say, 'But it was. It *was* easy.' Ease was a quality he prized; he saw it as something deeply positive. He had once gleefully told us an anecdote about Vladimir Horowitz who (allegedly) phoned a pianist friend late at night after a practice session and asked him whether he found it difficult to play a certain notorious passage. 'Yes', said the friend. 'I don't', replied Horowitz and put the phone down.

'We have to learn how not to fight against ourselves,' Sebök said once, 'because then we can fight against the real enemies.' I don't know who the real enemies were for him, or whether he had ever had any, but it was plain that he was not at war with himself. Unsurprisingly, in his self-sufficiency he cut a solitary figure. He didn't socialise with the students unless he had to. During the course in Ernen I used to wonder what he did in the evenings when all the students were meeting in bars and cafés. Whom did he socialise with? As far as we knew, he and his wife spent the evening in their chalet. Some professors deliberately maintain a kind of distance between themselves and their students, for the preservation of status, but I had the impression that it wouldn't even have occurred to Sebök to wander down to the bar to have a beer with any of us. I wasn't absolutely sure he would even have recognised us if we passed in the street. I imagined that in the evenings he read scientific books in the peace and quiet of his chalet, extracting concepts that might prove useful when analysing our problems or explaining why our solutions worked.

When I thought about all the advice he had given me from the first time I played to him in Canada, there was a thread running through it all, and the thread was having faith in my innate musicianship. To put it another way, he trusted me to find what was in the music, but he didn't want me to overlay the music's natural contours with intellectual thoughts of my own. He was sitting beside me once when I was playing Beethoven's last sonata for piano and violin in a class. I had drawn some up-and-down arrows on the score, indicating where I wanted the tension to rise and fall. He was reading the music over my shoulder, and in a voice so low that only I could hear, he said, 'Don't *give* it a shape. It *has* a shape.' In those few words he encapsulated the problem of interpretation. For no music can 'have a shape' unless someone plays it, and in sheer practical terms, when they do play it, they have to give it a shape because they are the one making the sound. I knew what he meant by the music 'having a shape', but when you are actually the pianist, where is the fine line between giving something a shape and allowing it to have its own shape? The moment you put your hands on the keys you become the composer's partner in creating the shape. Who is to say whether a performer is *giving* music a shape or letting it *have* a shape? Even the same performer might give different impressions to different members of the audience. In any case, I finally understood that my particular task was to trust my own musicianship. At first, that felt like being told that 'less is more', but it was, as he had said, more a case of knowing how not to fight against yourself.

As I started doing more teaching, I tried to follow Sebők's advice to 'collect information without prejudice'. I tried to emulate what he had said about 'opening the channel between his brain and his spine'. It worked, to some extent: I did find a way to sit back and simply let a person's playing register on me. However, I found that if I simply collected information without prejudice, I then had no particular wish to change anything in the person's playing. It was possible to sit quietly observing them and find myself thinking 'How interesting! They do this, and they don't do that.' But when I was in that state of mind, it felt like a one-way system. Information went in and was registered. If my goal was just to notice what was going on, that seemed incompatible with wishing to give the player any advice. In the context of 'giving a lesson' it felt inadequate just to observe, especially if the lesson was in front of an audience waiting to hear what I had to say when the student finished playing. As the teacher, I had to have something to add to the situation. Sebők had said one should try to make out what the player's 'dream' was, but half the time I thought the problem was that they didn't have one. Generally speaking, I felt that if the player genuinely had a vision of what they wanted to achieve, they were able to communicate that vision, despite technical problems.

If I was listening to someone who communicated mere accuracy and dutifulness, I found I had a strong desire to suggest to them what the next stage might be and how they might reach it. I could see what the dream *could* be, and I found that students were often appreciative if I described it to them. Their attention had often been entirely taken up with the challenge of mastering the notes, and it had left little room in their head for dreams. So I found that Sebök's 'objective observation' method was not ideal for me. It was perhaps partly because I was a woman, or at least, because I was perhaps more naturally interested than he was in what made individual students tick. He worked brilliantly with the symptoms, but I wanted to know more about the underlying causes. Unlike Sebök, I would always have enjoyed going for a coffee and discussing life, art and the cosmos with any of the students. I liked talking to them and I picked up clues from doing so, clues that fed into my ability to help them musically. Perhaps this meant that I was incapable of developing Sebök's Olympian detachment, but as I didn't have his temperament, any imitation would have been doomed to failure. In trying to emulate Sebök, I realised that I couldn't, but instead I discovered that I had my own way of doing things. I used to comfort myself by thinking that at least people could go and study with him if they wanted the direct experience. After he died in 1999, I began to feel that it was up to people like me, who had experienced his style of teaching, to try to preserve its essence in so far as anyone could. I think his strongest influence on my teaching style – and indeed on my writing – was his fearlessness in putting difficult things into words. Trying to follow his lead in that respect has been a satisfying task.

Once at a masterclass with Sebök in Utrecht, I asked him about this business of 'collecting information without prejudice'. I asked him how he managed to observe neutrally and still have a sense of what needed to be done. He seemed a little impatient with the question and merely replied that it wasn't a problem for him. At the time I thought he was stonewalling, but perhaps he wasn't. He once observed that 'objective love is the greatest love'. His audience of young musicians, all more or less embroiled at the time in love affairs of varying complexity, regarded that remark with scepticism and disbelief, but there was no doubt that he meant something important by it. He had mastered the art of 'objective distance', and I think his innate temperament was in his favour. I doubt whether he ever felt the rising anxiety that I often feel when listening to someone play in a masterclass and knowing that everyone is waiting to hear my response. 'Teaching is like improvisation', Sebök said once. 'It is like drawing a labyrinth. You have to take your pencil and start with a single point. At the beginning you are quite free. As you go on, you are more and more determined in your choice – and when the first response comes from the student, your path is yet more clear. But start with a basket of ideas, and try one after another until you get a positive response.'

Some of his most memorable sayings were like proverbs, and like proverbs they had a ring to them which made them seem almost like poetry. They may have been delivered matter-of-factly, but their meaning was far from ordinary. For example, I once heard him say to a student, 'You think being free is rocking from side to side or moving back and forth. But you should be able to sit perfectly still and feel free. Freedom is a big thing.'

Not all those who wander are lost

In Edinburgh's 'Cowgate', a dark medieval street which has had many changes of fortune over the centuries, there is a discreet little artwork in red neon lettering on the side of the Pilgrim Bar. It's a line from a poem by J.R.R. Tolkien: 'Not all those who wander are lost'. No doubt this line suggests different things to different people, but for me it evokes the spirit of jazz.

When you spend most of your time playing classical music, you are never 'lost' in the sense of not knowing what notes you should be playing. You may struggle with all kinds of things, but in classical music, at least since the nineteenth century, the notes themselves have been prescribed and are known to you and to everyone else who has ever looked at the score or heard the piece in question, just as the words of a Shakespeare play have been known and cherished for hundreds of years. There is in fact a long tradition of improvising in classical music, such as elaborating on continuo parts, devising embellishments, improvising descants, 'preluding' (creating little musical links between pieces in a concert) or even making up virtuosic solo cadenzas for concertos, but for a couple of hundred years now there has been a 'canon' of works whose notes, it is generally agreed, are not to be tampered with. At any rate, when I

179

was a student learning classical piano, nobody ever suggested I might improvise. Departing from the text was an impertinence.

In classical music there are many ways of creating or expressing a feeling of freedom, but 'wandering' would mean that you were not playing the right notes, and the right notes are the *sine qua non*, the 'without which, not'. If you do not play them, you are not playing the piece; you are not free to vary the actual notes according to your mood. The journey is laid out, and you know where you are going, so the 'wandering' is really concerned with how and to what effect. All this makes classical music profoundly different from jazz.

It's strange to think that I hardly came across jazz until I was at university, when a friend exhorted me to buy an LP of Django Reinhardt, Stéphane Grappelli and the Quintette du Hot Club de France, my first step in a rapid ascent to jazz fandom. I didn't really understand what jazz was or how it worked. I had just come across the wonderful light music of the 1920s piano virtuoso Billy Mayerl, whose music was fully notated, and I think I thought that jazz was just another type of light music, with the music similarly written down. It was a while before I understood that it wasn't. Jazz performers were improvising on a given set of 'chord changes' or a particular tune which might be only twelve bars long. After the tune had been stated, most of the rest was improvised, using the harmonic structure of the tune as a circular rail on which the whole thing ran round and round. When I did finally grasp that jazz musicians were 'making the music up as they went along', it seemed almost incredible. How on earth could they think so quickly? And if they were making it up, how come it sounded so secure?

As an audience gazes at us expectantly, waiting for the music to begin, all performers have to grapple with the disconcerting thought that there won't be any music if we don't play any. We are responsible for translating the music into sound, bringing music to life through our playing of instruments. For classical musicians this feeling has an underlying security because the music has already been composed; the musical score in front of us, or in our heads if we're playing from memory, maps out the minutes that stretch ahead. For jazz musicians the situation is different. Until we get to 'free jazz', most mainstream jazz uses harmonic structures which all the musicians are aware of, but there are no predetermined notes once improvising begins. There is no template to fall back on such as classical musicians have, so if jazz musicians cannot think of anything to play, there will be no music. In my early days of listening to jazz I found it entrancing that these musicians could not only think of something to play, but that it was often something so clever and amusing that it stuck in your head for ages afterwards.

I listened to the Quintette du Hot Club de France over and over again. The most memorable quality of that record was its *joie de vivre*. I loved the 'swing' they put into the phrases and the cutting edges of their rhythms. Their playing often seemed not just fun or entertaining, but joyful in a deeper sense. It was an important reminder to me that when we speak of 'playing' an instrument, the quality of 'play', as in having fun, should always be present. In my classical piano studies there were a great many satisfying elements, but sheer *fun* was not often one of them. How could I not love jazz? It brought me back to my senses.

At the time we students on the music degree course were studying historical performance practice and trying to understand what the old French theorists meant by advising musicians to play with 'notes inégales', the custom of playing pairs of notes of equal duration with a slightly unequal stress, the first note of each pair being longer than the second (it's a custom which is revived by 'authentic' period specialists, but hasn't survived in modern classical playing styles, or not that I know of). Reading the old treatises, it was hard to imagine the 'notes inégales' being played in a natural-sounding way. Why did they want to do that? Suddenly it struck me that the 'dooby-dooby-dooby-dooby' pairs of notes played by Reinhardt and Grappelli in their delightfully skipping jazz runs were probably just what the old theorists meant. I was charmed. Listening to this effect on the Hot Club de France disc, I felt some line running through history, connecting French musicians in wigs, brocade coats and buckle shoes to jazz players in the Gauloises-scented Parisian bars and clubs of the twentieth century. In a curious way, getting to know jazz at the same time as studying 'olden-day' performance practice helped me to see the line connecting seventeenth- and eighteenth-century musicians to my own contemporaries.

I was fascinated by the way that jazz invited freedom of improvisation on a strict framework of chords which all the players were following in their heads. First they played the tune or song on which they were going to improvise. Then the tune would disappear, but its underlying chords would be preserved as the tracks on which the next 'verses' would run. The tune itself might make occasional appearances as fragments in the improvised verses, but might be entirely absent until its return at the very end. What happened next could be described in a Zen-like way as 'the tuneless tune'. The listener could follow what was happening because the sequence of chords and the number of bars remained the same on each 'round'. I could see that creativity was sparked by the friction between ground-rules and freedom. The musicians weren't free to play just *anything*. They had to play something which would fit with what was going on underneath, which is far more demanding. It seemed a bit like the musical equivalent of doing a crossword, where things going 'across' (melodies) have to fit with things going 'down' (chords). The two things had to intersect, or the solution couldn't be correct. As there were endless numbers of tunes in jazz, musicians had to have excellent ears and memories. I was deeply impressed by their ability to conjure new elaborations while not losing track of the bar-by-bar harmonic changes. In fact, the best players' elaborations had the same elegance and impact as if they had been composed at leisure. It's always a test of a compelling phrase that it can be easily memorised. I found I could easily memorise Reinhardt's and Grappelli's improvised phrases. Maybe they *had* worked them out beforehand. If not, it was a truly remarkable skill.

Next I acquired a record of the jazz pianist Art Tatum, whose playing became as iconic for me as it was for eminent concert pianists like Rachmaninov and Horowitz who used to go to listen to him playing in New York jazz clubs in the 1930s. Tatum was blind, yet his touch was unbelievably sure. There was nothing tentative about the way he negotiated the piano keys. Though he was making things up on the spot, he never seemed to miss a step or 'play in the cracks' between the keys as ordinary pianists often did. I was used to anchoring myself by looking towards the piano key I wanted to jump to, but obviously Art Tatum wasn't doing that. He seemed to have a kind of 'perfect pitch' of space. His long, virtuosic runs from top to bottom of the keyboard were done with an effortless pearly perfection which recalled contemporary descriptions of Mozart's playing.

As a pianist myself I knew how hard it was to execute a long and perfect run at a lightning tempo, and I was astonished to hear this blind pianist doing it over and over again in any direction and in any key he liked, without giving any impression that he found it challenging. It seemed to indicate that there were types of 'security' beyond the ones I had been taught, which was a useful insight. Tatum was able to think at lightning speed while also executing the thought in the form of notes on the piano. He could improvise 'layers' of melody, harmony and decoration all going on at the same time in a way which misled many people who bought his records into thinking that there was some trickery afoot, such as multiple pianists pretending to be just one. Very likely Tatum *did* practise those 'snakes and ladders' runs with which he traversed the keyboard at top speed from treble to bass or vice versa, but the insouciance with which he threw them off, even when he was being recorded, was dazzling.

Tatum's style of jazz piano was not serious in character, but there was something about its playful generosity which seemed profound. To me, it brought a welcome message, one that was hard to put into words. It was something to do with the realisation that lightness of spirit and beauty of touch were not trivial things, but qualities of grace. The music probably struck me with particular force because of my own circumstances at the time. The year before I went to university, my mother had died of cancer after an illness of several years which devastated the family. I was still struggling to emerge from this traumatic period when I started at university, and its effects reverberated for years. To cut a long story short, I think I had gained some insight into how hard it was to put on a smile and go out to meet the world when you were bereft and sorrowful inside. Perhaps this is why I was so touched by the smiles-through-tears character of jazz. I had already discovered that there was much solace in the beautiful works of classical music which matched my mood, or portrayed a journey of introspection. What I hadn't encountered so much was the spirit of genuine playfulness and cheerfulness which jazz was able to conjure up, even (or perhaps especially) from musicians living lives of social deprivation. How could they walk away from their difficulties and play selflessly happy music which gave other people an hour or two of relief from their own problems? I could understand how one might immerse oneself in *sad* music. Choosing happy music was more complicated, but I sensed it was possible. It was a kind of music that seemed to *give* energy.

There are many similarities between jazz and classical music, because jazz is intellectually demanding and seems to be truly appreciated by a relatively small coterie of fans. At least, so I am told by professional jazz musicians who bewail the small audiences, small fees, and the difficulty of finding listeners who really know what they're listening to. Because of its origin in bars and clubs in New Orleans one might assume that jazz is an easy and popular form of entertainment, but it has moved a long way from its origins. These days only certain types of jazz have broad appeal, and they tend to be tuneful or 'historical' things like Dixieland bands, New Orleans jazz or early blues. As jazz moved through the twentieth century, into bebop, modal jazz, 'free jazz' and beyond, it became more of an acquired taste, with more adventurous harmonies, more overt seriousness and more specialised audiences who liked to follow in silence and with great concentration. It became well known that many of the jazz greats had struggled with issues of drug and alcohol abuse, and their music often contained more than a touch of pain. 'Modern jazz' has a fan base which has much in common with that of classical music: knowledgeable, serious, devoted.

Although there are dedicated jazz concerts, a lot of jazz is still hosted by bars and clubs where people go to talk, eat and drink as well as listen. Its tuneful background lulls people into feeling they can relax and talk freely without being overheard. For some jazz musicians and fans this is an irritation. If you go to bars where good jazz is played against a backdrop of people eating or having romantic dates, you can often see solitary jazz fans in attitudes of concentration, trying to wish away the drinkers and drown out the ambient noise of chat and cutlery so that they can follow every twist and turn of the music. Interestingly, when jazz moves out of the bar and into the concert hall, or into the dedicated space of a jazz club like Ronnie Scott's in London, jazz audiences often adopt the behaviour of classical ones, preserving a respectful quietness and, even if they bring their drinks into the hall, taking care only to clink glasses between pieces.

In my home town of Edinburgh I often go to hear the superb Scottish jazz pianist Brian Kellock who, as well as performing in jazz festivals and concerts, plays in one of the pubs on Sunday afternoons. Quite apart from his mastery of styles, Brian has a rare ability to devise long arcs of improvisation which sweep over several 'rounds' of the tune. When he starts building one of these spans, which can last for minutes, I love to witness how people stop talking, put down their glasses and cutlery, and give themselves up to its irresistible trajectory. I always think it must feel rather special to be able to make a roomful of people go quiet simply through the force of your musical thinking. In classical music you don't get the opportunity to hear silence descending on an audience like this, for it has become normal for classical concerts to be listened to in silence. Yes, one can often sense when a classical audience suddenly draws together in a shared intensity of concentration on what's happening on the platform, but that is a matter of distinguishing between different qualities of silence, or of attention.

During my university years, I don't think I ever went to a live jazz performance. In addition to academic study I was completely wrapped up in performing in my own student concerts (often more than one a week, plus rehearsals), and jazz events never crossed my radar. Jazz wasn't part of my degree course, and though my memory of the choices is hazy, I don't believe the study of jazz even existed as a module. Certainly nobody ever suggested that someone like me would be able to *play* it. When I left university and moved to London, my knowledge of jazz was more or less circumscribed by the records we had had in the college library. Some of the playing on these recordings was so polished-sounding that I didn't know whether they were really improvised or had been carefully worked out ahead of time, just like a classical composition. Naturally I had no idea whether the musicians were reading from written scores or not. I had never seen jazz musicians at work in a live setting.

In London, however, there was an enormous jazz scene. I started to go to certain pubs and cafés with a reputation for hosting serious jazz, and I saw musicians 'making it up on the spot'. Apart from the fact that almost all of them were men, they seemed to be British people pretty much like me. They weren't exotic creatures with a totally different musical background. It dawned on me that it might be possible for someone like me to learn to play jazz. Eventually I plucked up courage to ask some of the musicians about how one would learn to play it. They put me in touch with Howard Riley, one of the luminaries of the free jazz scene, who agreed to give me some lessons.

He began by showing me how the blues worked. He explained the traditional twelve-bar structure and its classic chord sequence, which was confined to simple chords of I-IV-V, or tonic, subdominant and dominant as classical musicians would call it. If you are in the key of C, this would mean chords of C, F and G. We began with the classic

'St Louis Blues', recorded by W.C. Handy and his band in 1922. So far, so familiar – I was used to playing by ear and quickly picked up the St Louis Blues. Howard and I played it a few times in duet, four hands on one piano, like verses of a folk song going round and round. But what next? Howard explained that we now moved into the territory of improvising. The chord sequence and the twelve-bar structure of the original St Louis Blues would remain. He would play its underlying harmonies as rhythmic chords in the piano's bass register, one per beat. But over the C major chord of the first two bars, I (sitting on his right at the keyboard) would play a note or notes that belonged to that chord. Over the next two bars, the F major chords, I would play notes that belonged to *those* harmonies, and so on. I need only play one 'appropriate' note per bar if I could only think of one. If I could think of more than one, I should play them, but they must be drawn from the underlying harmonies. He would keep time and play the twelve-bar chord sequence over and over, without waiting for me if I got in a muddle. If I couldn't think of any suitable notes to play, I should wait until the next chord change and see if I could play a note or two there. Off we went, Howard playing in the bass and me in the treble. I was a highly trained musician, but I was amazed by how disconcerting it was to have to invent the notes 'in real time', without falling behind in rhythm or making my partner wait for me.

Many of my favourite composers were very fond of 'theme and variation' form, and I had memorised quite a few such works, relishing the composers' ability to use the harmonic structure of the theme or its melodic shape and to make them step forth in new costumes. So for me there was nothing new about the idea that the blues was another example of variation form. The big difference was that in all the works I had studied, the variations had been composed by *someone else*, someone brilliant who had taken time to work them out in the privacy of their composing studio. Their variations were works of intellectual achievement, not spur-of-the moment ideas composed in 'real time'. I was not a composer. As a student I had done my share of harmony and counterpoint lessons, and had tried my hand at writing variations, but I probably had a week to write them. I could sketch things in, erase them, throw them away, start from scratch. I had time to reflect, time to try things out on the piano, time to find better solutions, to write them down note by note. That was very different from being required to *produce*, on the spur of the moment, new variations in time to the rhythmic blues chords which ticked away mercilessly under my teacher's hands, daring me to fall behind. Making things up at leisure was one thing. Making them up *in tempo* was another.

I shouldn't go overboard and pretend this exercise was *entirely* new to me, because any trained musician should be able to supply plausible harmonies to go with a bass line. It's the task facing anyone setting out to 'realise' a figured bass, the Baroque tradition of supplying a bass line and a system of numbers and symbols (such as sharps and flats) indicating what chords should be played with any given note. Any keyboard player who has played Baroque chamber music will have tried their hand at putting chords, and ideally something more interesting than just chords, to a given bass. Good harpsichordists can join those chords up with linking melodic phrases and embellishments. With sufficient notice of what piece is to be played, a keyboard player can work out appropriate chords and practise embellishing phrases in advance, but skilful players can make them up on the spot, even working in musical motifs from other instrumental lines, and adding to the music's character by their choice of how lightly or densely to add melody and harmony to the bass. The task is similar to, but in other ways not the same as playing jazz, because usually a figured bass part in Baroque music is an accompanying part. In practice (if played on a harpsichord, say) it is often semi-audible amongst the louder, more sustaining instruments of a Baroque ensemble. If a keyboard part is intended to be heard in every detail, as for example in a harpsichord concerto, it is usually not left to chance, but is written out by the composer.

So when my jazz teacher sat down next to me and played just

the chords of the twelve-bar blues, I did know how to supply 'context-appropriate' notes above those chords. What was much more difficult, though, was to improvise *connections* between those notes as the chords passed by. If I simply rattled up and down the arpeggios derived from the chords in the bass, the resulting treble part was no more than a zigzag series of dots. They suggested no overarching phrase or line to lead the ear onwards. I quickly saw that a higher order of invention was needed if there was going to be a chance of creating a pleasing melodic counterpart to the bass. Rapidly I discovered the difference between a sequence of notes which remain stubbornly separate from one another, and a sequence of notes which link together in the listener's mind to become a unit or a melodic phrase. In classical repertoire I had often reflected on the mystery of what makes 'a melodic line' as opposed to a row of individual notes, a difference quite subtle and hard to define, and a judgement which in any case we might not all agree on. In the attempt to improvise a pleasing line over the top of my teacher's blues chords, I was forced to consider the magic formula which enables notes to 'connect'. Was it really possible to improvise melodies on the spur of the moment in response to a given sequence of chords? Some jazz musicians could do it, as I had heard for myself.

In a nutshell, this is what distinguishes a good jazz musician from a plodding one. I often listen to American jazz radio while I'm working in the kitchen, and every night I hear far more examples of dull, formulaic playing than I do of fresh, inventive improvisation. With good understanding of harmony it is not difficult to play something acceptable, but it turns out to be very difficult to improvise a line which knits the notes together in a beautiful and persuasive way. Equally rare is to be able to play with true judgement and restraint (as distinct from lack of imagination). There are some instruments – for example the saxophone – whose straightforward fingering seems to tempt players into blurting out too many notes. Naturally the best saxophone players don't fall into this trap, but there are many who over-embroider the tunes simply because it is easy to do so. I must admit that in this respect the piano can also be a culprit.

In order to create a melodic unit, jazz musicians need to have a sense of where they are heading and where they can introduce notes that do not belong to the underlying chord. In traditional jazz the matter of which notes 'belong to the chord' is a bit different from, say, Baroque music, because in jazz the seventh of the chord (usually the flat seventh) is taken for granted practically as much as the third and fifth of the chord. When I first started playing jazz I found it a curious sensation to end a piece on a seventh chord, which felt somehow unstable or unfinished, but I gradually tuned in to the language of jazz and learned to hear the seventh chord as conclusive.

My jazz teacher in London also ran a jazz piano evening class, which I joined. Everyone was a serious jazz fan, but I was the only trained classical pianist. The rest of them were much more knowledgeable about jazz repertoire than I was. We took it in turn to improvise in front of one another, and it was in this setting that I made the discovery that my 'superior' piano technique was considered a liability. Fellow classmates put it to me that my technique was holding me back. It was all too easy (they said) for me to run up and down the keyboard in impressive arpeggios which made it sound as if I was thinking fast when I actually wasn't. They thought I should slow down and play a few well-chosen thoughtful notes rather than 120 notes on automatic pilot. There was some truth to this. I had noticed that when nervous or unsure what to play, I could fill in the empty beats with filigree figuration, rather as the Russian violinist Nathan Milstein had done at my friend's lesson. This was considered cheating by my classmates in the jazz evening class. I was only half-impressed by their moral seriousness, because I had an inkling that their attitude was partly a rationalisation of the fact that their own piano techniques were not up to whizzing around the keyboard. There was just one respect in which they acknowledged that my classical technique put me ahead of the game, and that was when improvising solos with the left hand only. Everyone else found it very hard to move fluently around the bass register with their left hand, but for me as for any accomplished classical pianist, zooming about with the left hand was 'meat and drink'. I didn't find it hard, for example, to imitate with my left hand the kind of jazz solo a double bass player might play. My classmates, whose left-hand piano playing was mainly confined to playing chords on the beat, acknowledged that I had the edge in the matter of left-hand solos, but they still maintained that I played 'too many notes'.

The difficulty and virtuosity of music written for the piano in classical music, not to mention its emotional depth and variety, means that a pianist has to develop very sophisticated technical skills simply to be able to play what has been written for the instrument. The notes were prescribed; there was no leeway not to play them. If a page of transcendent virtuosity appeared in front of me, I couldn't decide to skip over it, count a few bars in silence, and join in again when there was something simpler. If I was in a reflective mood, I couldn't decide to 'précis' the composer's music and offer just a few notes indicative of my mental state. If I was in boisterous mood, I wasn't free to obliterate a slow movement with crashing dissonances, outbursts of fast notes, or disjointed 'commentary'.

All this was very different from jazz, where only the chord sequence was given. In jazz it was perfectly possible to give a serious contribution by playing very little, as for example Miles Davis sometimes did. You could utterly change the character of the music, for example taking a slow ballad and turning it into a raucous display. You could slow down a cheery Broadway number and sour it with unexpected dissonances and silences. Nobody would ever accuse you of not having played the right notes in the improvised verses, because none were indicated. It was up to you to decide what notes to play, which gave you incredible freedom, but also offered the possibility to reveal yourself as someone with limited imagination if you couldn't come up with anything interesting. It was a totally different kind of challenge compared to classical music. In classical, we were always trying to be more and more accurate, more faithful to the score, better at memorising it, readier for any technical demands made on us by the composer. Their written notes were non-negotiable.

In jazz, on the other hand, we had to use our judgement about when to play, what to play, how much to play or whether to play at all. The freedom was not absolute, but was firmly tied to the harmonic sequence of whatever tune we were improvising on, which made for a unique and hopefully creative tension between what was 'given' and what was expected of the musician (how to fill the next few minutes with freshly minted music). Naturally it is hard to be always fresh and inventive. Most jazz musicians practise ahead of time the *sort of things* they will play when they find themselves in front of an audience; it's just a practical way to approach the task. If players are able to agree ahead of time what tunes they will be playing, they sometimes work out *exactly* what they plan to play when it is their turn to do a solo. In a performance one can often recognise such sections of 'prepared improvisation', which have the quality of something baked rather than a bunch of ingredients being stirred in front of you, and are often no less satisfying for having been cooked up in the peace and quiet of the player's studio.

There's a kind of medicine cabinet of runs, twirls, arpeggios and decorations that can be relied upon as 'fillers' if musicians' minds go blank. Jazz musicians speak of 'practising their chops', which means building up the technical ability to move around their instrument, but also seems to include amassing a repertoire of musical procedures that can be used as the building blocks of improvisations. There seem to be 'typical' gestures that belong to specific instruments; the pealing top-to-bottom runs of the saxophone, for example, or the delicate widely-spaced pizzicato arpeggios of the double bass. Almost everyone needs these gestures to fall back on, because it is simply not possible that you will *always* be able to invent never-before-heard and compelling music in real time while other musicians are playing along with you. Nearly everyone needs the musical equivalent of the TV presenter's 'here's one I made earlier'. Often when listening to jazz one can hear a player clinging desperately to the original tune as the 'verses' go round and round, playing it over and over with almost no variation, unable to tear themselves away and launch into the unknown. We're meant to think they're improvising, though they clearly aren't.

There's another very big difference between classical and jazz players: in classical, the huge treasury of performances on record acts as a kind of 'global standard'. There's a whole industry of commentary and comparison on the different performances, reflecting on why they are different and what effect the differences have. Each musician who makes a record hopes that their own particular interpretation of the music will provide a new and fruitful angle on it, one that will bring them fans. They hope that their new recording will be spoken of in the same breath as Sviatoslav Richter's or Claudio Arrau's. Yet they have to play exactly the same notes as every other pianist who has ever recorded the work since recording began over a century ago. The differences are not in the notes but in the sound, the character, the tempo, the way the transitions are handled, and the cultural attitude on display.

In jazz, by contrast, no self-respecting musician would wish to play exactly what any other musician had played except as a formal exercise or as a conscious tribute or 'recreation'. What would be the point? The aim is to respond newly and *now* in one's own special way. You can buy books of music in which people have diligently transcribed, say, exactly the notes that Erroll Garner or Bill Evans played on such-and-such a record. It's very interesting to study such transcriptions, to get a glimpse of what it would feel like to be that musician, how their mind worked, what size their hands must have been. Musicians do study them and learn to play them to broaden their knowledge of what could be done. But to go in front of the public and regurgitate that transcription would be regarded as a pointless thing to do, at least for a serious jazz musician. You might attract a certain specialised audience if you declared it was a 'homage to Bill Evans' or whatever, but otherwise you would simply be wasting an opportunity to do your own thing.

This is not to say that all jazz musicians are creative geniuses. Jazz may be about playfulness and freedom, but as in any other art form there's a whole spectrum of accomplishment, from musicians who can do no better than regurgitate tired old formulas, to players who seem able to mould the time and shape the phrases with their own unique authority. Some of my most boring live music events have been spent listening to jazz groups with nothing fresh to say. But at the top end of the spectrum, those rare players who can think and react 'on the wing' are, for me, as admirable and skilful as the best classical artists.

One of the things I loved about classical music was that it brought me into contact with the great musical minds of the past. Their works were not spur-of-the-moment inspirations to be enjoyed and forgotten, but rather slowly matured, intricate meditations which mirrored the forms of our thinking and feeling. I felt that there was always going to be a difference between music made up on the spur of the moment (as in improvising) and music that was sculpted and burnished by someone with deep mastery of composition. Beethoven, for example, spoke of 'seeing his music in front of him as though cast', meaning that in his imagination it was like a three-dimensional object (I believe Mozart said something similar about his own work). The masterworks of such powerful minds seemed to me different from the linear, volatile improvisations of jazz, no matter how brilliant. It was just a different kind of thing: like comparing a great Renaissance oil painting with a marvellous cartoon in today's newspaper. Much as I admired the skill of good jazz musicians, I had never heard anything improvised which matched the depth of music crafted patiently in solitude by a genius. The classical composers I admired had powers beyond mine and that is what made their music worthy of long and patient study. It was a privilege to fulfil their expectations, and when you managed to play great music as it was intended to be heard, it gave you great intellectual and spiritual satisfaction.

Jazz, on the other hand, offered a chance to wrestle with musical inspiration itself. It was a feeling of being in contact with the raw materials of time and sound. Disconcertingly, it was also an opportunity to observe your own brain at work. The moment when one finished playing the 'tune' and launched out into unscripted improvisation was a bit like walking along a diving-board and then jumping off into empty air. Much of the work of preparing a classical performance was to do with exploration and choice of tone colour, touch and singing qualities. As we studied the music in advance, we knew what its moods and range of expression were, and could prepare for them. There was a vast palette of instrumental tone to be searched through to find a match for any given emotion or expression, and that search was the bread-and-butter of a classical musician's practice sessions.

Playing jazz was therefore a very different feeling. As the musical time flew by, invention and execution had to be in harness; your task was not only to invent notes to play, but to play them as you were inventing them. To separate these two tasks (inventing and playing) may sound pedantic, but of course you can 'hear' things in your head without playing them, and much of classical music is based on pieces which someone heard in their head and then handed over to someone else to sing or play. Playing things without 'hearing' them in your head is also possible, as I had discovered in my evening class when nervousness propelled my fingers into playing an excess of scales and arpeggios. When I watch a really fine jazz musician at work, I wish I could see a graph of their neurological activity, for I feel that there must be an unusual amount of brain power being used. Inventing music away from the instrument (as many classical composers do) is an imaginative skill which, as we know, can lead to very great works of art. Inventing music on the instrument, while keeping in time with other players and with a rhythmically inflexible set of harmonic changes, is a physical skill as well as a mental one.

One day, when I had been set to practise improvising on a certain tune, I tried making up an improvisation by walking about the room, humming and 'scat singing' in an elementary way. Then I sat down and improvised on the piano. I was astounded to discover that the two sets of improvisations were quite different. It was almost as though my vocal improvising came from a different part of my brain than my instrumental improvising. Obviously my technique came into it: my 'humming improvisation' was simple and melodic, within a fairly narrow compass of intervals, whereas my piano improvisation was faster and more complex, with counterpoint, lots of leaping about, and interesting rhythms. Yet it wasn't just that my instrumental technique was better than my vocal technique; it was that right from the start, different notes occurred to me when I was singing than when I was playing. 'Vocal me' seemed to have a different musical personality from 'instrumental me'. This was a fascinating discovery and made me think more deeply about why I used my hands the way I did.

It also made me think more deeply about why ideas emerge as they do in different artistic mediums. It may seem banal to say that the artistic medium has a big influence on what is expressed, but after realising that singing and playing were two different routes into/out of my brain, I saw with more awareness how the tools and techniques of other art forms dictated what could be expressed, or not. For example, many artists have given us their impression of rain. But Hokusai's delicate woodblock prints of rain falling on bridges and fields, Debussy's musical impressions of rain (e.g. 'Jardins sous la pluie') and Charles Dickens's literary description of rainy London streets are all indissolubly linked to the medium of expression. It appeared that even my own way of improvising on the jazz tune 'Here's That Rainy Day' would differ according to whether I was singing, playing the piano, playing my violin or playing a drum – not because my bank of thoughts and memories of rain shifted as I changed instrument, but because the different tools and materials made the change happen automatically, without my conscious intervention. The violin bow as opposed to the drumstick, the human voice as distinct from the piano keys – these tools had a powerful influence. The medium shapes the artist's thoughts and suggests a way of proceeding, but might also put obstacles in the way of expressing certain things. I suppose for example that a sculptor might have difficulty in rendering the look and feel of rain in marble.

I began to have an insight into why classical pianists have a different physical style of playing from jazz pianists. I had always assumed that pianists were able to use graceful arm movements because they did not have to hold or lift their instrument, and were therefore free to use naturally flowing movements in the space above and around the keyboard. But now I saw it was also related to the type of music. Classical pianists knew what they were going to be playing and had had time to consider things like arm choreography and perhaps also body language that would illuminate the musical meaning or add something to it. As they practised how to approach each note and phrase, they evolved a wide repertoire of gestures to go with them, such as attacking the key from far away, or moving sideways along the keys with superb legato fingering. Jazz pianists, on the other hand, needed to stay close to the keys in order to be near enough to play any note which popped into their head. There was no advantage in swaying from side to side or making sweeping gestures of the hands or arms, because all such movements risked separating you from the keys. All the excellent jazz pianists I've seen have used a very economical, undemonstrative technique, sitting still and staying close to the keys, rarely using the kind of lift-and-drop technique often seen in classical pianism. They never seemed to send their arms on graceful curves through the air to 'link' one phrase to another. I started to see why. If you had to invent each note, it would be madness to be prevented from playing it because your hands were up in the air. The physical language of the jazz player was therefore very different from the physical language of the classical concert pianist. When I started learning to play jazz, I found myself switching from the one 'register' to the other quite naturally, but the two were very distinct from one another and almost made me feel like a different sort of musician.

I noticed too that jazz pianists didn't seem to use the 'thumb under' technique which is such a major part of classical piano playing. For example, in a C major scale of one octave, a pianist would usually play the first three notes with thumb, index finger, middle finger, and would then pass their thumb under those two fingers to play the fourth note in the scale, effectively re-positioning the hand so that all five fingers are available to finish the scale. If you don't pass the thumb under, but simply play the first five notes of the scale with fingers 1-2-3-4-5, you're then obliged to 'hop' with your hand to arrive higher up the keyboard for the next notes. Classical pianists practise the 'thumb under' as a pivot, a way of creating a legato line, and they spend a lot of time working out the fingering, writing it above the relevant notes in the score so that they know where the thumb is going to be 'passed under'. Jazz pianists don't seem to do this and I suppose it is linked to the fact that they don't know in advance what notes they're going to play or have the opportunity to work out the fingering beforehand. Creating a smooth legato line is less of a preoccupation in jazz. This is not to deprecate the ability of the good jazz pianist to get around the keyboard, because many of them have astonishing fluency, but if you watch them closely you'll probably see that their hands 'hop' around the keyboard very economically, without using the 'thumb under' method.

When my jazz teacher felt I was making progress, he suggested I might think of going to the US to do some further study. I was actually trying to establish myself as a pianist and chamber musician on the London scene, but things were being slow to get started, and I thought I could slip away for a few months while other projects were 'cooking'. Howard Riley much admired the jazz pianist Jaki Byard, who taught at the New England Conservatory in Boston. Howard suggested I look into getting some scholarship money to go there. At that time, however, I had just become enamoured of the playing of jazz pianist Bill Evans, whose records Howard had introduced me to in my lessons, saying that he thought they would appeal to me (and how right he was). Bill Evans played with a wonderful poise and delicacy, a beautiful touch, a very sophisticated choice of chord spacings, and an enviable ability to create melodic phrases. He had great musical judgement and was one of the rare jazz pianists who didn't seem to use 'too many notes'. I replied that I would rather go to New York and study with Bill Evans. Howard made enquiries, but we found that Bill Evans didn't have a teaching position, and possibly didn't teach at all. We hatched a plan that I would apply to Boston, but if and when I made it to the States I would write to Bill Evans and persuade him to give me some private lessons. In the days before the internet, we had no idea how to find out where Bill Evans lived, but we agreed that once I got to Boston and started to meet people in the jazz world, it wouldn't be too hard to find out his address. In the meantime, if I was to apply for scholarship money, it seemed sensible to apply to a recognised course at a top institution. I bought an LP of Jaki Byard and realised that he was a terrific pianist. His daring, eccentric style was very different from mine but I felt I would learn a lot from such an adventurous musician.

I discovered that the New England Conservatory offered a sort of part-time 'associate student' option which didn't require me to enrol on a full course, but would enable me to have individual lessons for a semester, as well as joining in with some ensemble activities. This was the most affordable option and didn't commit me to staying for longer than a few months. It took me about a year to organise everything, but I did manage to get together a term's worth of money. In the process I had some interesting experiences, because my applications were to music scholarship funds set up primarily for programmes of classical study. I knew them because I had applied to them myself in the past for classical projects. They were surprised to find me asking for money to study jazz, but they agreed to hear me. And so it was that I found myself on stage in London's Wigmore Hall, improvising on 'Someday My Prince Will Come', Frank Churchill's famous song from the 1937 Disney *Snow White*, on a magnificent Steinway in front of an august panel of the great and good. I had played classical concerts many times in the hall, but it was a slightly surreal experience to be playing jazz there (this was long before the hall offered jazz concerts). One of the panellists saw me in the foyer afterwards and said how much he'd enjoyed it. 'Where did you find the transcription?' he asked. 'It wasn't a transcription', I said. 'I was improvising on the song.' He looked puzzled. 'But presumably you had written it all down?' he said. 'Well, no. I was making it up as I went along. I didn't make up the song itself, obviously, but all the rest was improvised', I said; 'that's what jazz is.' He looked thunderstruck. 'You were making it up on the spot?' he said. 'Good Heavens!' Clearly I wasn't the only one who had a lot to learn about jazz.

In 1980 I travelled to Boston to study jazz piano for one semester. Perhaps foolishly, I decided not even to make contact with the classical department of the Conservatory. I didn't want to get sucked into playing for other people's lessons, as had always happened at the other colleges I'd been involved with. I was only going to be there for four months, and I didn't want my time there to be defined in any way by my classical persona: it was going to be all about jazz. (This, I now realise, was typical of my 'purist' and not very pragmatic approach.) My teacher, Jaki Byard, was a large and imposing African-American with a shock of black hair, a hearty laugh and a penetrating gaze. He seemed to be diverted by my appearance in his class as an escapee from the world of classical piano. At one of my very first lessons, he said to me, 'Man! Ain't it a shame about Bill Evans!' 'What's happened?' I asked anxiously. 'He died!' said Jaki. 'It was in the paper yesterday. Didn't you see?' I hadn't been buying American newspapers, and my lodgings didn't have a radio or TV, so I hadn't heard. I was stunned. Bill Evans, my jazz idol! I couldn't believe that he had gone. And now, although I was closer than I'd ever been to New York, I would never have the chance to meet him or play to him. It threw a shadow over my stay in the States.

Jaki was really a performer, with a big name on the New York jazz scene, but he was also committed to education. His method of teaching was similar to Howard Riley's duet method, except that instead of playing 'four hands' on one upright piano, we played on two grand pianos side by side in Jaki's studio. He sat at one, and the student sat at the other. We would agree on a tune, sometimes there and then, but usually a week in advance so that I could practise improvising on it. Then at my lesson we would play it in duet, taking it in turns to improvise a solo while the other one played the chord changes. It was a challenging but fast way to learn. When I was playing the chord changes, Jaki would swoop off into his solo improvisation at the other piano, crashing up and down the keyboard with his dramatic flights of fancy. I listened with terror, knowing that in twelve, twenty-four or thirty-six bars' time (depending on how many times he decided to 'go round' the tune) it would be my turn to take over as soloist while he played the chord changes for me. Not much was put into words; it was all done by demonstration and listening. If he was pleased with me, he would shout out congratulations while we played.

Jaki was a virtuoso pianist himself and seemed to find it fun to have a student whose technique was as fluent as mine. If he wasn't pleased, he would accompany me wordlessly, waiting for his turn to show me how it could be done. He never 'let me win' like a tactful sportsman who underplays for the benefit of a beginner. This was probably a good policy because it drove up the standard of my playing. It took strong nerves to learn in this fashion, but it was also very inspiring, because naturally I did my best not to let him down when it was my turn to take the lead. It's difficult to design a good jazz improvisation by speaking about it, so just doing it and giving me the opportunity to be part of it was probably the most valuable thing he could have done. I developed a better grasp of the 'formulas' a player can use to weave a web of sound over a sequence of chords, and started to sound more plausibly like a jazz pianist. I didn't any longer have that terrified walking-off-the-plank feeling, because I had a repertoire of phrases to use. Nevertheless, the challenge of thinking in long units remained enormous, especially when the chord changes were complex and hard to memorise. Jaki could 'build' a solo which took several verses of the tune to play itself out, but I had only the occasional glimpse of what it was like to be able to do that. Jazz musicians who had mastered long-range thinking, like Charlie Parker and John Coltrane, went up even more in my estimation.

I had thought that going to the States as an 'associate student' was a smart strategy because it saved me an enormous amount on fees. However, I hadn't thoroughly taken on board that being a part-timer, not studying for a particular course, would mean that I didn't qualify to take part in many of the things automatically offered to full-time students. As a mere 'associate', I didn't pay a lot of money, but conversely the institution didn't have to look after me. Clearly I had not reflected sufficiently on my experience some years earlier as a private student of Vlado Perlemuter in Paris (again on a small grant which just paid for a term's lessons). Because I had felt so isolated in Paris, I had resolved never again to study somewhere where I had no easy built-in way of meeting people. This time, by attaching myself to a music conservatory, I imagined I was taking care of 'the loneliness problem', but it turned out that being allowed to have my lessons in the building was not the same as being part of a social scene. It wasn't the institution's fault – it was my own decision to be a 'bird of passage', not even there for a whole academic year. Most students lived across the street in the 'student dorm'; I was lodging privately in a Boston suburb. My landlords were nice, but extremely busy. Although I was allowed to practise in college if I could find an empty room, I wasn't following a structured course on which I would automatically meet other students, so I spent a lot of time on my own. I spent hours listening to jazz records on headphones in the library. I bought a guidebook and set out each weekend to explore a different part of the city on foot. I read books on a lot of park benches, eating cream-cheese bagels, watching passers-by and storing up Bostonian vignettes to relay in airmail letters to friends back home. They faithfully wrote back and I took their letters on my walks to re-read. In the spirit of research I sought out interesting jazz artists and went to jazz bars to hear them, but found that it wasn't altogether enjoyable or advisable to spend evenings in such bars on my own.

Alongside my individual lessons, I was randomly assigned to a student jazz group for weekly sessions, rehearsing on our own. This wasn't a happy experience. Jaki had never given the slightest sign that he didn't think I fitted in to the jazz world. But the group of young American men I was assigned to play with seemed to think otherwise. They were not pleased to find that their pianist was a shy British woman, classically trained, conservatively dressed by their fashion standards, a glasses-wearing intellectual who was only going to be in the US for a few months. I didn't talk the right talk, didn't smoke or take drugs, didn't arrive casually half an hour late for rehearsals like they did. I didn't go straight from rehearsals to the bar down the street. They said I 'sounded too classical' when I played, and if I used words like 'episode' or 'recapitulation' they looked away as if embarrassed. They talked among themselves in an American slang I couldn't even attempt to imitate. For example, the saxophone players referred to their instruments as 'axes', a jazz slang dating back to the 1950s. To me this had an aggressive, macho ring I couldn't empathise with.

It was strange and discouraging to be in a collaborative musical situation where I felt I couldn't fit in. I was so used to feeling at home in chamber music groups – 'but that was in another country', as Shakespeare would say. When we came to a stop during our jazz rehearsals, I followed my usual custom of trying to suggest what we might change or improve. This didn't go down well either. Speaking aloud was already a sign that you weren't 'in the groove', and if anyone was going to speak, it wasn't going to be the one woman. There was a pretence that if the vibe was right, nobody needed to say anything: inspiration would take care of itself. I found this a little hypocritical because as I wandered round the corridors looking for practice rooms, I would hear the saxophone players earnestly practising the 'breaks' or solo passages which they later produced 'as if inspired' in rehearsal. I felt there was an element of reverse snobbery in their attitude to me. Perhaps they were secretly worried that I would look down on them, and so they adopted the defensive position of looking down on me first. We in the classical music scene are often told that classical music is 'intimidating' because it seems to have 'mysterious rules' about how to behave, rules that make you feel small if you don't know them. Now I discovered that jazz had its mysterious rules too – rules I didn't understand.

I came to dread our sessions. Before long, the group fizzled out – partly because they all knew I was going home at Christmas, and they didn't see the point of investing time in sorting anything out. Looking back on it, I think I was just unlucky with the particular mix of people. Knowing what I know now about how such things are organised, I presume that a part-time 'associate student' didn't qualify for one of the better groups intended to last through the whole year or longer. Jaki said, 'Aw, forget them. Just do your own thing.' But I felt I had come up against an invisible barrier. Was it maybe true that I didn't fit in to the jazz scene?

Everyone says that music is a universal language, but when it comes to being a performer amongst other performers, different kinds of music have their own cultures and expectations, almost their own entry requirements. Musical genres have their roots in different countries, *raisons d'être* and social backgrounds. Along with the music comes a set of attitudes, a way of proceeding, almost a lifestyle. Any music fan can shuffle between different kinds of recorded music and swap freely between the genres without restrictions. However, for a player it's not so easy to swap between different musical scenes. Yes, I had learned to play a bit of jazz, but that didn't mean I had gained entry to the world of jazz musicians. I daresay my difficulties would have been mirrored by the experiences of, say, an experienced jazz violinist who out of the blue decided to spend a few months at a classical conservatoire as a member of a string quartet working on Haydn and Beethoven. As it happens, I know quite a few classically-trained instrumentalists who are good at playing jazz as well. But I don't know any who slip effortlessly from one world to another. In one world they are at home. In the other, they are a visitor, maybe even welcome as a guest, but not to be taken for a permanent resident.

One of the differences was the issue of drug-taking. It was well known that many of the greatest jazz musicians had drug habits. I was aware that Bill Evans was a heroin addict, and so were many of his colleagues. Years later, I heard a radio programme in which Bill Evans's playing was analysed as showing the typical state of consciousness of the heroin user: the pinpoint awareness, the sense of time slowing down enough that you could control tiny parts of it, the search for transcendence. I had interpreted all these qualities as characteristic of *him*, not of his drug use, and so they were, of course, but there was clearly an ingredient that was beyond my comprehension. That sense of an expanded awareness of time was characteristic of other great jazz players too. I started to wonder whether the long-range improvising skills of musicians like Charlie Parker and John Coltrane were also dependent to some extent on the mental acuity produced by drugs. Bill Evans's case surprised me more because he was a pianist and therefore expected to produce multi-layered ambidextrous music with melody, counterpoint, and harmony as well as rhythmic accompaniment. I was astonished to learn that it was possible to play so gracefully when under the influence of drugs. Most of my musician friends, careful of their hard-won playing skills, deliberately avoided anything stronger than wine and beer. We had all been practising our instruments every day since we were children, training for what we hoped would be successful careers. It seemed crazy to jeopardise all that hard-won expertise. I had noticed that after a glass of wine, my sense of fine motor control in my fingers was slightly muted, so I banned myself from having a drink until after a performance, a custom I have managed to stick to. The same was true of most of my colleagues, though I have one or two who feel they play better after a relaxing beer (none of them are pianists). At any rate, for professional reasons we were all wary of the effects of anything stronger. I was never tempted to experiment, and I realise I was fortunate in not being in a milieu where I was driven to experiment. The case of Bill Evans seemed to show that it was possible to retain your playing ability and even to sharpen your improvising skills, as Evans was said to have done in his last few troubled years. Certainly soft drug use was prevalent on the jazz scene when I was a student. I wasn't involved in it, and that was perhaps another reason I didn't fit in socially.

In 1999 the Open University ran a radio series on 'Gender and Music' for which they interviewed leading jazz players such as saxophone player Barbara Thompson, who formed her own group Paraphernalia, and American jazz lecturer and pianist José Bowen. Almost twenty years after I went to Boston, their opening question was, 'Why are there so few women jazz *players* when there are so many women singers?' Answering this question, José Bowen referred to the 'very male' competitive atmosphere amongst jazz musicians. He mentioned the so-called 'cutting competitions' of the 1940s and 1950s in which jazz musicians (male) would try to play faster, louder, higher than anyone else on the platform. This was called 'cutting' other musicians, an interesting choice of word in itself, even if it simply referred to 'cutting in'. (It reminded me unpleasantly of the jazz word 'axe' for a musical instrument.) Women were never encouraged to adopt these competitive attitudes or ways of behaving in public, and even if they had been invited on to the platform for a 'cutting competition', might have found it disagreeable to play in such a macho atmosphere. 'There is built into the art form a tendency towards aggression', Bowen commented, going on to say (perhaps sarcastically) that, 'in some ways the field was wide open for women if we can get past the social difficulties involved, the hours, and the attitude on the bandstand'. Today there are a number of brilliant women jazz pianists such as Carla Bley, Diana Krall and Norah Jones, but if you look up lists of women jazz pianists over the past century you're likely to be surprised by how few of them you've ever heard of – even of the ones active today. Barbara Thompson, who entered the jazz world professionally in the 1970s, reached the conclusion that, faced with the macho atmosphere amongst instrumentalists, women 'might want an easier life. Women aren't stupid. I always laugh – sometimes I go to Ronnie Scott's and they're very tough guys, they're really strong, you know, and you wouldn't like to meet them on a dark night.' It was clear that women instrumentalists, if they were to thrive in the jazz world, would have to create their own conditions and not simply try to be 'one of the boys'.

When I got to the end of the semester, having spent a great deal of time on my own, I was quite glad to be going home. Jaki Byard was the only person I was sad to say goodbye to. At my last lesson he said something very touching: 'You're the kind of person who doesn't really need a teacher, because you have something inside you that will just go on unfolding and unfolding whether anyone is pushing you to learn new things or not. You'll just keep moving ahead.' This meant a lot to me, particularly as he only knew me as a jazz pianist. Like all the best 'mentor' advice, it gave me something to aspire to as well. In the time to come, whenever I felt too lazy to tackle something new, I often remembered Jaki Byard having said that I would 'go on unfolding', and I didn't want him to have been wrong.

Back in London, I found that some of my classical projects had been 'cooking' nicely. My group Domus was making lots of plans for travels and performances in the summer. I was warmly welcomed back and felt the relief of being able to fit in with my musical colleagues. Their way of working seemed perfectly aligned with mine. It all came as a great weight off my mind. To prove to myself that my time in America had been of benefit, I did make myself go in for a jazz competition, the Greater London Arts Association's 'Young Jazz Musician of the Year'. This was an award with several winners each year, and that year I was one of the winners as a solo pianist. The prize led to some informal invitations to 'sit in' with people like the pianist Denis Rose in his regular gig in Camden Market, and it led to a few solo jazz gigs in cafés and bars where

I discovered the perils of trying to play while people smoked, drank, talked and moved around. After the quiet concentration of the classical audience, the noise and distraction of the typical jazz venue was hard to get used to. I remember playing one night in a South Bank wine bar where, if I stopped for too long, the manager would sidle up to the piano and ask me not to leave such long gaps between numbers, because the silence made the customers feel uncomfortable. Could I just keep playing? It was actually very tiring to keep playing continuously, or at least it was for me, especially if I was trying to be inventive. There were no other players around me to take the strain or give me a break. I was playing all the time just to guarantee being in the background. Was this really a way forward for me? There were also challenges involved in being a lone woman on the jazz scene. I still loved jazz, but there were things about its lifestyle I felt I could never learn to love. By contrast, my group Domus was raring to go. Everyone was idealistic; everyone wanted to throw themselves into rehearsal, and I felt a big part of it all. I felt myself being sucked back into the world of classical music.

In the years that followed, Domus became an all-consuming project. As I've described elsewhere (particularly in *Beyond the Notes*), I was very active as an administrator as well as a performer, and it turned into a more than full-time job. As my life with Domus became more and more absorbing, my semester of American jazz seemed to become a distant memory. At least, I couldn't see a path that led forwards from it. It began to feel as if it had been a 'gap year' project. Occasionally I played a jazz gig in our portable geodesic dome, sometimes with guest performers such as bassist Roger Dean or vocalist Maggie Nichols. Both of them were interested in 'free jazz', an extension of what I had studied, and I tried to learn its language. It was so far removed from the world of, say, Louis Armstrong that they didn't really use a framework of traditional 'chord changes', or of predictable phrase-lengths or numbers of bars. Their aim was to create a musical narrative on the spur of the moment, playing whatever musical gesture seemed appropriate as a response to the one that had gone before. Someone would fling a musical suggestion into the pot, and someone else would answer it, or perhaps contradict it. Sometimes everyone would be playing at once, to create density or an impression of activity. We never knew or planned whether a piece would last for two minutes or twenty. 'Openness' and 'energy' were paramount, and although sometimes we used recognisable jazz harmonies, we also turned our backs on them for long periods, playing anything from 'clusters' to widely-spaced dissonances. We might treat the instruments in an unorthodox manner, too, for example playing rhythmic patterns on the lid of the piano keyboard or on the body of the double bass. Rehearsals were only of 'the type of thing' we might play in the concert, for obviously we couldn't fix anything beforehand without losing its spontaneity. The point was to do something new. For a classical musician, it was disconcerting territory. In rehearsal, Maggie was struck by how difficult it was for me to wait in the cloud of unknowing. She said she noticed that if I didn't know what to play, I nevertheless felt compelled to play *something*. I remember her saying to me compassionately during one rehearsal, 'You're not very good at being lost, are you?' I couldn't help reflecting that such an observation would make no sense in the context of a classical music rehearsal, where 'being lost' would not be a good thing. It was true: in my life as a classical pianist I was used to finding, and playing things that were found. I wanted to be found too.

Roger Dean and I once played a modern/free jazz concert at Nottingham University, where I had already performed several times as a classical pianist. Roger was a pianist as well as a double bass player and for the jazz event we played duets on two pianos, Roger playing a digital piano and me a Steinway acoustic piano. After the concert there was a 'feedback event' where the professor of music led a discussion with students. He commented that when listening to me play jazz, he missed the sense of enormous attention to tone colour and touch which he recalled from my classical concerts. He had remembered me as a pianist with a characteristically warm and thoughtful sound. That sound, he now told me, was missing from my jazz playing, which seemed spiky and dry. I wasn't using the range of beautiful tone colours offered by the Steinway grand piano. He wondered if that was deliberate? I was taken aback. It was true that because I was playing duets with a digital piano it seemed appropriate to use a drier touch, but I didn't like to hear that my sound wasn't warm and thoughtful any more. I can't remember if I found anything to say in my defence at the time, but reflecting on it later I realised that when playing jazz my priorities were indeed different. As there were no notes ready-made for me, my focus was on deciding *what* notes to play and what rhythms to play them in. That task absorbed so much of my attention that the choice of precise tone colours or pianistic touch seemed like a luxury, something I had insufficient time to consider. Selection of pitches and durations seemed by far the most urgent task. By contrast, when playing classical music, the pitches had already been selected and I was free to give my attention to exactly how I was going to play them. No doubt there are jazz pianists who are able to give their attention to matters of touch and tone, but with most of the jazz pianists I've ever listened to, it's not so much *how* but *what* they choose to play which is most striking.

When I went to the States to study jazz, my intention was to create a sort of double-track career in which I played both jazz and classical, swapping between the two as I liked. It didn't work out like that, but not really because I rejected the idea. Jazz has often been associated with music of protest, music of grievance, and even though it has moved a long way from its origins in the American South, there is still a strong, almost 'tribal' feeling that jazz belongs to, or ought to be represented by, people who don't fit in elsewhere and who look to one another for validation. I realised that feeling comfortable in the jazz world involved much more than simply knowing the tunes and being able to play the music. Whether this was a real or imagined problem, I felt I was always on the outside looking in to the jazz community. This was not the case with the classical music world, where many more of my colleagues were women, and I felt accepted for myself. Decisions about whether to pursue any sort of jazz career were in any case swept out of my hands by the sudden increase in my classical commitments when I got back to London. As I got busier, I found that I was once again sitting in the audience listening to jazz, rather than aspiring to be on stage playing jazz myself.

Thanks to my jazz studies, however, I understood it much better. When I was a young member of the National Youth Orchestra of Great Britain, playing my violin, we were memorably conducted by Pierre Boulez who told us one day in rehearsal that although most of us would not become professional musicians, we would be the 'expert listeners' of the future, the knowledgeable and empathetic audiences for whom professional musicians yearn. We would know from personal experience exactly what was involved and why it is so difficult to reach a really high level. Performers would be thankful to have us in the audience. I realised that, as far as jazz was concerned, I had turned into the kind of listener that Boulez meant. I had always enjoyed listening to jazz but my pleasure now had an added dimension of understanding, and also of admiration, for I now properly appreciated how difficult it is to be a really fine jazz musician. I knew what was involved, or what should be involved, and I could follow every twist and turn in my imagination, trying to guess what would happen next and often 'playing along' with the performer in my head. In my view, jazz as we usually see it in bars and pubs is just masquerading as a casual, slightly scruffy, harmless entertainment. It's really a form of heightened awareness akin to Zen Buddhism, and its best exponents are masters.

The sound of two hands clapping

I like most types of music, but from time to time my interest is powerfully caught by a particular kind of music which seems to call out to me. It's more than simply finding something interesting; it's more like what the French call 'coup de foudre', the lightning strike which tells you that you've fallen in love. The thing that ignites my interest seems to stand out in relief from the world around it with a special numinous quality. Whenever this happens, I pay attention, because there's usually a deeper reason for the attraction. I feel I'm meant to learn something from it.

Some years ago, on a trip to Seville, I went to a flamenco performance at the Casa de la Memoria. Flamenco dancers, gorgeously costumed and groomed, are the best-known public face of flamenco, but on this occasion it wasn't the dancing which particularly struck me, nor even the singers or guitarists, no matter how splendid they were. What really caught my attention was the soberly-clad musicians doing the 'palmas', or rhythmic clapping which seemed to anchor everything else. The 'palmeros' sat in a small semicircle of musicians with the singer, guitarist and cajón (a hollow resonating box) player. Their clapping was like the heartbeat of the whole team. The patterns they clapped were hugely sophisticated.

They had a variety of techniques to create different dynamics, and in between the claps they used gentle 'gliding' movements to fill the silent beats by sliding the palms past one another. They used intriguing non-western hand gestures to show the ends of certain phrases or cycles, almost as an Indian classical dancer might. I felt I was hearing something rooted far away in history and geography. Ignorantly, I had thought of flamenco as a form of 'entertainment', but an evening of watching the 'palmeros' gave me a glimpse into its seriousness. I knew little of its social origins but I could immediately appreciate its *musical* intensity.

Over the years I had thought quite a lot about the sound of clapping. Ever since someone advised me that it was calming to listen to the sound of the audience clapping as one walked on stage, I had made a habit of listening to the characteristic sound that each audience makes when it applauds. In classical music, people don't 'clap along' to the music, but in other forms of music, such as folk or pop, 'clapping along' to the beat is a way for listeners to participate. It tends to be done in a somewhat haphazard way. In fact, when listening to popular music I often had to shut out the sound of people clapping along because it distracted me to hear the ragged volley of claps that clustered around the beat. Clapping was, in my experience, usually an unfocused sort of sound. Until I went to that first flamenco performance, I had never seen or heard clapping elevated to an art form.

As a pianist, I was used to playing both melody and rhythmic accompaniment, often at the same time. I was well aware of the importance of steady rhythm to keep the other musicians on the beat, and I enjoyed being able to provide it. When I was a teenager I learned percussion instruments as my third study after piano and violin, and I played percussion in the National Youth Orchestra of Great Britain. Later I became good enough to do extra work as a percussionist with professional orchestras when I was a student. So my attraction to percussion wasn't new. But for most of the percussion instruments I had learned – timpani, side drum, xylophone, vibraphone, gong, bass drum, tubular bells – the instruments were played with sticks. The percussive sound was literally at arm's length. When I considered the matter, I realised that the same is true of playing the piano; the hands are used to operate a mechanism which causes a hammer to strike a string somewhere in the piano's interior. The sound doesn't come out of the hands themselves. So it felt different to see and hear *the hands themselves* used as percussion instruments.

Part of my fascination was bafflement. As a trained musician I was good at rhythm and counting, but the patterns they were counting in flamenco were new to me. Each type of dance seemed to have its own pattern. I could hear that most of the dances had a twelve-count pattern, and the twelve beats were divided into groups of twos and threes in various permutations, but beyond that there was a complexity which dazzled me. Why did they start where they were starting, stop where they were stopping? Why was there such decisive emphasis of certain unusual beats? Why were some beats left empty and how did everyone know where those empty beats were going to be? I was fascinated too by the way a pair of 'palmeros' (clapping musicians) would subdivide the beats between them, one playing on the beat and the other on the half-beat. In fast music, their ability to clap on the half-beat was stunningly accurate. As I listened I realised that these volleys of half-beat exchanges occurred only at certain phases of the dance, not all the way through. But what was the recipe for where they occurred? How did they know when to change from one pattern to another during a long dance sequence? I couldn't work it out. It was strange not to know, as though I were listening to people talking a different language.

After my holiday was over, I found that while the memory of the dancers faded away, the fascination of the 'palmas' stayed with me. I wanted to know more. Next time a renowned flamenco show came to London, I went to see it. Of course I am not blind to the beauty of flamenco dancing, but once again I was fascinated by the palmas. I saw that in addition to the main 'palmeros', the other performers, including the singers and the dancers, also joined in with the clapping from time to time. I realised that in flamenco there was a different balance of power between melody, harmony and rhythm. In classical music, one might argue about whether melody or harmony is the most important thing, but most of us would agree that melody and harmony are the two prime ingredients. Naturally melody and harmony cannot exist without rhythm, but rhythm plays a less prominent role than melody and harmony in western art music. In flamenco, it seemed to me that *rhythm* was the primary element, which actually made it feel profoundly different. Of course there were melody and harmony too, but the balance was subtly altered. There were songs, and lyrics (usually passionate laments), virtuosic guitar playing and the fabulous spectacle of the dancers in their 'traje de flamenca' outfits, beating out complicated staccato patterns with their surprisingly sturdy low-heeled dance shoes on the wooden floor. But the heart of the matter was the driving rhythm, and the heart of the rhythm was the clapping. I couldn't take my eyes off the palmeros who, seated quietly among the instrumentalists, seemed to be the power behind the throne, the engines of the music. I felt like a watchmaker who has been given the opportunity to look inside an elegant watch to see how it actually works.

There was something about this elevation of rhythm to the top spot that made me want to explore the art of palmas. My interest at that point had very little to do with the cultural side of flamenco. I didn't speak Spanish (though I later started learning it). I knew almost nothing of the long tradition of flamenco, its beliefs and its roots in different regions of Andalucía. I knew nothing of its most revered performers and for which qualities they were revered. The passionate, usually male singing which formed the opening section of each 'number' was rather too melodramatic for my taste. Even the dancing, though it was lovely to watch, was of secondary interest to me. My attraction was purely musical. I recognised something in the rhythms and patterns that appealed to me on a deep musical level, and that would have been so even if the dancing, the guitar playing and the singing were taken away. In classical music I was used to counting silently as I played, 'dropping the beats into the background'. In flamenco, the rhythms, or one could say the bones of the music, were brought right into the foreground. Wikipedia says that 'good palmas can be a substitute for music', but I sensed that the word 'substitute' was misleading; good palmas *was* music. It could be *the* music. The other things were embroidery.

I tried to find out if there were amateur classes I could attend. I was living in London, where it is not difficult to find any kind of class you want, but the flamenco schools told me they would only offer palmas lessons as an adjunct to flamenco dance classes, so I would have to sign up for dance classes first. Actually, this didn't interest me and I knew that my friends would choke on their toast at the idea of me as a flamenco dancer. I just loved the palmas rhythms and wanted to learn how they worked. It didn't seem possible to learn that in isolation, so I put the notion aside. Some years later, I moved to Edinburgh. By then, I had forgotten about the idea of learning palmas. But my lovely daughter Maya hadn't forgotten and she managed to find out that, amazingly, there was a small flamenco school, Alba Flamenca ('Alba' is the Gaelic word for Scotland), not far from my new home. Even better, they had a palmas class on a Saturday afternoon and were happy to let me join it without also enrolling for dance classes. As a birthday present, Maya bought me a course of classes, one of the most satisfying presents I ever received.

In the summer prior to the classes, I went along to see one of the flamenco shows put on by the tutors. Their building was in a little backstreet, their studio about the size of my living-room. The tiny stage just had room for a dancer, a guitarist, a cajón player, and two singers who doubled as *palmeros*, or perhaps it was the other way round. The performing space was barely half a dozen steps wide and the whole thing looked rather ramshackle. My expectations were low, because I have been to a great many performances of 'world music' which have had more enthusiasm than skill. But as soon as they started to play I was jolted awake. In fact, I felt that shock of relief and gratitude that I always experience on encountering performers who are masters of their art. (Being a perfectionist isn't often fun, but it does mean that when you see very high-level achievement, you are truly in a position to appreciate it.) Their ensemble and rhythmic control were fabulous, their performing style full of spirit and heart. They displayed a level of engagement with the music which I would love to have been able to bottle and later pour into the ears of my classical piano students. To my way of thinking the pair of singers, male and female, who also did the 'palmas' were the best of the lot. What were they doing in an Edinburgh backstreet? It was thrilling to realise that there was a little flamenco enclave just up the road from where I lived.

In the autumn I started attending the palmas class at Alba Flamenca. To my delight I found that my teacher was Inma, the singer and 'palmista' of the show I had attended. We were a mixed bunch of pupils: a social worker, a science researcher, a history professor, a teacher of Argentine tango, a drum-obsessed teenager, a van driver, and a woman recovering from a neurological illness. To my surprise, one of my fellow pupils was a dancer from the show. I had seen her clapping complicated rhythms in the performance, so I asked her why she had come along to the class. She told me she had learned certain rhythms as part of her dance routine but had never really understood the principles underlying them. She wanted to improve her familiarity with the 'compás', or basic rhythms. She observed that the palmas was 'the most difficult part of flamenco' and that only really good musicians could master it. 'We depend on them, totally', she said in a humble tone that I found striking from someone I had seen twirling glamorously in a red and black flamenco dress in front of an enthralled audience. I couldn't help wondering how many classical ballet dancers would ever sit in on a piano rehearsal in their free time, just to improve their familiarity with the music.

Being in the palmas class was a most unusual experience for me because everything was done by ear. Not a single thing was written down, and no 'classical' music terminology was used by the tutor.

This did not mean that she didn't know exactly what she was doing, but she didn't analyse it in any of the ways I was used to, and if I ever asked questions using the analytical vocabulary I knew, she didn't recognise the terms. We did everything in Spanish, not easy for me as I didn't speak any Spanish at the time. The complex patterns of alegrías, bulerías, seguiriyas and so on had to be memorised and remembered from class to class, because they were never notated, and I never saw a note of written music in the flamenco school. I had never tried to learn without being able to look at some printed music; even in jazz there was often a basic chord chart to refer to. But in flamenco there was nothing. Our teacher had everything in her head and expected us to do likewise. She demonstrated, and we copied her. I felt curiously insecure without anything to remind me what we'd done, and after classes I sometimes used to sit on a doorstep in the street and try to notate the patterns we'd learned on whatever scraps of paper I happened to have in my bag.

The way I notated them made sense to me but wouldn't have meant anything to someone brought up in the flamenco tradition, because they have a different conception of the musical metre. Right at the start of our classes I got a tremendous intellectual shock when I discovered that they counted the music in a different way. Instead of counting the way I was used to – e.g. 1, 2, 3, 4 – they had a counting system more analogous to that of a clock face. *Twelve*, not one, was the first important stress. In flamenco, a twelve-beat pattern was the one most commonly encountered. The twelve beats were subdivided into groups of three and two, typically two groups of three, and three of two. So far, so easy – but the method of counting them was very different. To understand it, I had to visualise an old-fashioned round clock face. They began with an upbeat to the twelve (obviously, this was eleven). If we were doing a pattern of two groups of three beats followed by three groups of two beats, it would be counted and stressed as follows: 'eleven **twelve** one two **three** four five **six** seven **eight** nine **ten**'. We counted in Spanish. As the Spanish words for 11 and 12, 'once' and 'doce' (pronounced

219

on-thay and doh-thay), were too long to say quickly, they said 'un' and 'dos' instead of 'once' and 'doce'. Then they said 'un' and 'dos' again to signify 1 and 2. So the twelve-beat pattern would go, 'un **dos** un dos **tres** cuatro cinco **seis** siete **ocho** nueve **diez**'.

It's hard to convey how confusing I found this at first. I told Inma, our teacher, 'I can't count like this. I'm going to have to count in the way I know.' 'Please don't', she replied. 'If you count in any other way but this, you will never know what I mean when I say that we are now going to clap on three, six and ten – or on one, three, and five. You *have* to count the same way that I am counting.' After a brief but strenuous spell in which I tried to listen to her counting 'flamenco style' while I secretly counted 'classical style' in my head, I saw she was right. It was counterproductive to have a secret parallel system. So I started trying to hear the flamenco patterns as starting with the 'eleven, twelve' of the clock face. When I did finally get used to it, and the counting felt natural, I enjoyed counting in that way. I never did figure out why the different counting method made the patterns *feel* different. They could have been counted in the 'classical' way, and sometimes I did that just for interest, but the 'clock face' method had some subtle effect on the way I perceived the patterns. Our patterns generally ended with a decisive snap on the count of *ten*. In my classical way of counting this would have been eleven. Just a way of counting, you might think, but in some peculiar way there was more satisfaction to be gained from ending on *ten*. In fact, for me there was general satisfaction in ending phrases so decisively. In classical music I often found myself pleading with students to shape the ends of their phrases properly and not let them simply trail weakly away. Of course there are many types of phrases and many ways of ending them, but in flamenco class I never got tired of the joyous way that musical phrases launched themselves at their final note.

There were two main sounds in palmas: soft and strong. I was fine with the soft (*sordas*), but Inma was not pleased with my attempts to do *fuerte* (strong) clapping. I did my best to copy her, but she kept complaining that my clapping was feeble. Rhythmically I was correct, but the actual sound was too pale for her liking. She kept trying to show me the way to hold my hands so that when we were doing the 'fuertes', I could make a properly loud and resonant sound. I found this surprisingly hard, almost as if I were being asked to go beyond a certain boundary I didn't know I had set. It seemed that my own estimate of 'loud clapping' was not the same as hers. Even when I felt I was clapping loudly, she kept saying, 'Susan! More!' Eventually I did manage to make the correct sound, but whenever I stopped concentrating it would fall back to a gentler style, earning me a reproachful look. I felt I was carrying over from my classical training an assumption that to bang out the beats was elementary, something you should leave behind as soon as you were able to make a long, smooth line. In flamenco, there was a different sort of emphasis.

Of course the best musicians tried to make long phrases, as they would in any art form, but the strong beats were never required to fade tactfully into the background. When the dancers got going with their staccato footwork, this delight in hammering out the beats and fractions of beats was very clear. A ballet-trained friend of mine had commented that classical ballet was all about 'up': up on the toes, up in the air, leaving the ground, balancing on one leg with the other high in the air. It was an art of defying gravity. Flamenco was the opposite. There were no arabesques, almost no jumping. No matter what graceful shapes the dancers made with their upper bodies, they didn't seem at all interested in leaving the ground. Contact with the ground, stamping on the floor, hammering out patterns on the earth, *being grounded* – this was the glory of flamenco. It was not 'up, up, up' but 'down, down, down'. Even the vocal lines seemed to start high and descend. At the virtuosic climax of dances, the dancers would bunch their skirts up into their hands to reveal their legs from the knees down, and would turn to face us so that we could concentrate on the sight and sound of their feet pounding the stage for the final minutes of the dance. Defying gravity wasn't part of the aesthetic: it was a love affair with the earth.

'Fuerte' clapping was part of this aesthetic. I was almost reluctant to clap as hard as my teacher wanted me to, in case it damaged my hands for classical playing. Furthermore I couldn't help feeling that were I to hear someone attack the piano keys with the same degree of vehemence, it would repel me. But here there was no alternative: 'fuerte' was a vital part of the idiom and if I wasn't prepared to do it, I might as well stop going to the classes. Banging out the beats was not 'childish' but proud and masterful. I had seen Inma clapping with great 'attack' in the shows and I knew there must be a technique which maximised the sound without using excessive force (there was: it was partly a question of holding the fingers of the right hand in a certain way against the taut left palm). I sensed that the snap of the beats, the stamping, the 'fuerte' palmas were all expressions of a culture I could only really observe as an outsider. Inma had directed me to look at certain videos of famous flamenco performers old and young; watching them, their body language and their way of interacting with one another I realised that in some respects it was a style that, no matter how much I loved it *musically*, would remain a closed book to me culturally. However, I knew from experience that if you cannot approach something from the inside, you can sometimes get surprisingly far by approaching it from the outside in. In this case, it meant copying the idioms and outward signs of flamenco culture as manifested in excellent 'palmas' technique, to see if it led to a corresponding inward feeling. And actually, it did; copying the outward signs produced some 'sympathetic vibrations' in me which were meaningful.

Our palmas class gradually became quite good at the various 'compás' or rhythmic patterns which characterised the dance types. As the weeks went on we ventured upon 'contrapalmas', the thrilling half-beat clapping which can be done at various phases of the dance, often to provide rhythmic excitement towards the end of a phrase. This was a very interesting stage of the class, because it demonstrated how beat-bound we are in our society. Many people in the class had great trouble with the task of intervening between the beats. They could clap *on* the beat very confidently, but when asked to clap on the half-beat they were on shaky ground. We did a lot of exercises where we didn't clap on the beat at all, but only on the half-beats. Then we took it in turns to clap *on* the beat while another person clapped *between* the beats. We did asymmetrical patterns where we would clap on certain strong beats but remain silent for others, then clap on the half-beat only as we approached the end of the phrase (always ending on *ten!*).

I grew familiar with the puzzled look on my classmates' faces as they tried to find the right moment to intervene with a half-beat. It was evident that they didn't really have a clear guideline in their heads of how to do it, and it sometimes felt almost as if the concept of 'the space between the beats' was new to them. Often they would lean forward and try to snap at the imaginary half-beat as if it were a butterfly hovering out of reach. When they leaned forward like this, I had the impression that they conceived of the musical pulse as being something outside of themselves, something they had to capture and bring within their orbit. I felt more at home with the task because I was used to thinking of rhythms as being part of me, already in my imagination, not something separate from me. I was also used to subdividing beats in any number of complicated ways. I was itching to be asked to explain the method to the class, but I also realised that we were all, me included, meant to be learning something in the way that students might learn it in a flamenco class in Spain. This was an oral tradition. Occasionally when someone asked me how a rhythmic pattern worked, I would explain in standard classical music terms (crotchet, quaver, barline, rest, tie, syncopation), but it felt strange to be doing so in a context where no 'western art music' vocabulary was ever used. I knew that our teacher had probably learned entirely by ear from someone who had learned by ear themselves. She was a brilliant demonstrator, but when someone asked her to explain something, her answer was to show them again, more slowly and with bigger gestures.

Analytical vocabulary seemed both sorely needed and wholly out of place. I wondered how I would fare if I was doing all this for the first time by ear. I found that I was automatically working out how to notate whatever we were being asked to do. Once I had done this, I felt more secure. As it happened, I had a good memory and didn't find it hard to remember rhythmic patterns, but recalling them a week or a month later, or after the holidays, was quite challenging. Often I had to whip out the scrap of paper on which I'd written down a previous week's exercise and put it on the floor beside me so that I could read it as I clapped. To use such an *aide-mémoire* felt a bit like cheating. On the one hand, it gave me a failsafe way of recalling the patterns. On the other hand it made me realise how dependent I had always been on notation. It was as if when I saw something written down I understood it better. This was a moment of self-discovery for me and one that I didn't entirely enjoy. My admiration for our teacher, who never seemed to have the slightest trouble recalling anything, was unbounded.

Perhaps one reason why my scraps of paper seemed out of place was that flamenco seemed to have nothing to do with composers. The forms of the dances were ancient and passed down by watching the older generation do them. I suppose that long ago there were individuals who made the dances up and taught them to others, but knowledge of who they were had long been lost; the forms and rhythms belonged to the community. There was never any talk of 'so-and-so's bulería' or 'so-and-so's alegría'. There were no texts to study and interpret. This made it feel utterly different from classical music, and different even from jazz where the starting point is usually some particular composer's song. The point of flamenco was to do it, to take part in it, to use your musicianship to create something living and fresh. But this certainly didn't mean that there was nothing to get right. On the contrary, respect for tradition ensured that there was enormous attention to detail on the part of everyone involved: singers, guitarists, dancers, cajonists, palmeros. Accuracy was crucial for the proper functioning of the different dance forms and their rhythmic structures. But it was perfectionism of a different kind.

In classical music I was accustomed to asking myself what Beethoven or Schubert *really meant* by writing this or that. I had looked at every note and every instruction, as had countless other musicians before me. In flamenco there was no particular composer's vision to serve, but there *was* an intricate pattern to get right. Getting it right meant developing a very reliable sense of rhythm so that the performers always knew where the beats and half-beats were, even at the fastest tempos. A properly functioning bulería (for example) was like a beautiful piece of clockwork. If your task was to enter the fray with a volley of clapping on the half-beats when the speed was at its height, it was impossible to do so with the required brilliance unless your partners were absolutely accurate with their beats. Adrenalin often makes people speed up in performance, and we discovered that we had to fight against this effect if the rhythmic integrity was to be maintained. It was no good having (or being) a nervous partner who let the tempo run ahead. When I watched Inma and her partner Danielo in performance I was struck by their tight control over the musical pulse – a control that many classical performers might envy.

Having played concerts in Spain, I had realised that the Spanish attitude to time was more relaxed than ours, or at any rate very different. Concerts often began late, sometimes very late, and everyone seemed to take this for granted. The same was true of the flamenco team in Edinburgh; Spanish customs did not lose their force even though the local audience were in their seats promptly for the advertised start time. I found it fascinating to observe the difference between the relaxed way the flamenco performers drifted on to the stage, and then the way they suddenly launched themselves into a blazing rhythmic display, subdividing the beats with stunning precision. For me, there is no difference between starting a meeting at 2 p.m. sharp and being punctual on the downbeat of a piano trio. I like to be what Scottish lawyers call 'timeous' both in music and in everyday life, though admittedly that may be as much a matter of temperament as of training. As a member of the audience at flamenco 'noches' I had to realise that for them, clock time and musical time each had their own realms, which reflected very different ways of counting.

I never saw any sign of them 'preparing mentally' for the performance in the way that I and my classical colleagues did, practising up until the moment it was time to go on stage. They seemed utterly relaxed until the moment the music started. The only parallel I had seen in the classical world was when as a teenager I was given the chance to turn pages for Daniel Barenboim and Pinchas Zukerman when they played a duo recital at the Usher Hall during the Edinburgh International Festival. When I arrived in the 'green room' beforehand to be instructed about the page-turns, there was no sign of them practising or meditating on what was to come (as I had been taught to do). Instead, they were laughing and joking, and they continued to laugh and joke all the way up the stairs to the stage door and even as they walked across the platform. Walking behind with the piano music, I observed them with wonder. I could hardly imagine being so insouciant that one could still be telling the punchline of a joke to the sound of ecstatic applause. Of course, they were acclaimed performers at the height of their powers. Why shouldn't they be as nonchalant as they liked? It all seemed very different from the serious, methodical way I had been taught to approach an important concert.

I had read that Fritz Kreisler, considered the greatest violinist of his day, disliked practising and would sometimes rely on the opening section of a recital to 'warm up'. His audiences in the early years of the twentieth century got to know that his best playing would happen later in the programme. "I have worked a great deal in my life, but have always found that too large an amount of purely technique work fatigued me and reacted unfavourably on my imagination', Kreisler wrote. 'It has often done me more good to dip my fingertips in hot water for a few seconds before stepping out on the platform than to spend a couple of hours practising.' This indicated a very different attitude, redolent of a different era. My fellow music students and I had been taught that first impressions were everything and that as a matter of simple respect for the audience, one should start every concert at full throttle. Why in any case would one *not* want to play one's best straightaway, after all that practice? But occasionally stories like Kreisler's would give me pause. Perhaps the performance manners I had been taught were simply 'of their time', as Kreisler's seemed to me? Maybe warming up on stage was pleasantly human and would be understood as such by a forgiving audience? Whatever the truth of the matter, I did not feel I could ever bring myself to use the first half of a solo recital to 'get going'.

I was struck by the difference between a genre like classical music, which revolves around the performance and interpretation of written texts, and flamenco which (like many dance forms around the world) is improvised around a set of long-familiar guidelines. Sometimes I felt a little sad that 'my' type of music was one which depended on composers and written texts. Classical music without the composer was as unthinkable as classical ballet without the choreographer. I reflected that if a visitor from Mars were to ask a group of classical musicians to play something to illustrate what classical music was, they would first need to go and get some printed music in order to play a piece written by someone else. The same would be true with classical ballet – a group of dancers would need to agree on which memorised section of which ballet to perform. They wouldn't just pirouette randomly about the stage doing arabesques and pliés wherever they felt like it – that would be a different dance style altogether. But if the Martian visitor asked what a flamenco alegría was like, even a beginner like me could immediately beat out the essential rhythm which defined its style.

On the one hand I recognised that the classical tradition, with its emphasis on notation and its cult of solitary composers, had enabled the development of music of great complexity and intellectual depth. The astounding quality of this music was what had kept me loyal to it over the years. Its written tradition also ensured the preservation of music from centuries ago which we were able to reconstruct and perform. By contrast, flamenco's lack of a written heritage meant that nothing was more complex than could be devised by the people involved in the performance. This is not to disparage things made up on the spur of the moment, which as I knew from watching their 'noches' could be mesmerising. But the emphasis was on spirit and commitment, not intellectual depth. And although we now have an archive of a century of flamenco on film and sound recordings, we will never know exactly what long-ago flamenco artists actually played or how they performed; their music was not transmitted to us by notation. The beauty of flamenco was its freshness and transience as well as the immediate spectacle.

Because of my classical training I was in some ways at an advantage in the class, but my advantage shrank when we practised using our feet as percussion instruments, as is often done in flamenco. Sometimes we'd be asked to stamp out certain beats or half-beats with the foot, while clapping others with the hands. When Inma demonstrated this, she lifted her whole foot from the floor and could bang it down at any tempo. At slow speeds I found it possible to use my whole foot, but as the speed increased, my foot seemed to become deaf to the instructions from my brain. (Curiously, it was the opposite for some of the 'advanced' flamenco dancers learning palmas along with us. They could stand up and beat out fast rhythms with their feet, but found it challenging to capture those same rhythms with their hands.) My hands could match the increase in speed without any problem, but at faster speeds my foot became sluggish, like the foot of an unmusical person. It was an infuriating sensation. I had once read that if you tapped a dinosaur on the tail, it would take seconds for the dinosaur to turn its head to see what you were doing. I felt as if I was half-dinosaur at those moments.

I mentioned my unmusical foot one day to a friend trained in classical ballet. He said it was hardly surprising that my feet were 'slow' because they had never been trained in rhythmic movement. If I knew exactly where I was rhythmically, my foot wasn't 'unmusical' but merely untrained. Short of taking up dance training, which he supposed would cure the problem, he suggested that I might try resting part of the foot on the floor and tapping with the other part, as fewer muscles would be needed. I tried resting the heel on the floor and tapping with the toe, but I still found this strenuous and eventually discovered that it worked better if I rested the toe on the floor and tapped with the heel. I also realised that if I was in any way using my feet for balance – for example if I was sitting too far forward on the stool – it was impossible to move my feet fast enough to be punctual on the half-beats. The experience of having a sluggish foot made me realise that when other members of the class lunged wildly at half-beats with their hands they might be thinking the right thing but not reacting physically fast enough.

We began to memorise quite complex sequences in which, like in jazz, we went round and round a twelve-beat pattern with 'verses' which got more and more complicated. Syncopations and rests were introduced to create more interest and tension. We added verse to verse until we had quite a long chain, and we clapped our way through the sequence over and over. My favourite moments were those where it was my turn to perform the contrapalmas (between-the-beats) rhythms, which required fast reflexes. If one of the 'advanced' dancers was taking part in the class, she would get up and show us certain dance steps so that we could practise, for example, keeping pace with her as she speeded up through the virtuoso 'cadenza' at the end of a dance. Sometimes our teacher would sing us an Andalucían song so we could practise clapping to it. Apart from that, our classes were pure percussion. One could see the 'entrainment' theory at work. When they were called upon to perform parts of the sequence on their own, individual members of the class would falter and make mistakes, but when we were all clapping together we sounded remarkably unified and competent.

I found that at the end of an hour of concentrated rhythmic clapping I felt curiously energised. When we emerged from the building into the little lane, I often felt quite buoyant, as if through our clapping we had tapped into some primitive energy source. For me this was a new and intriguing sensation. I was used to feeling energised by a good chamber music rehearsal, but that was a lot to do with the sensation of being swept along on wonderful melodic and harmonic waves together with other people. The palmas class was 'just rhythm', which I guess I had thought of as being merely an ingredient in a more complex musical whole, but it turned out there was nothing 'merely' about it. The rhythms on their own, delivered with wholehearted engagement, were a powerful force with radiating effects. In the intervals between the classes these rhythms started to take up residence in my head, and their pulses interacted with my own. I was used to melodies, or melodies-plus-harmonies, populating my imagination but I now began to realise that 'pure rhythm' was equally worth contemplating. At any rate I found I could get as much intellectual nourishment from 'chewing over' *compás* rhythms as I did from following the contours of, say, a Schubert melody. When I thought about the rhythms I felt the kind of satisfaction that I imagine a biologist would get from looking through a microscope and seeing the particles our world is made of.

It took me months to get thoroughly used to the flamenco way of counting, but I did finally get used to it and find it natural. Therefore my intellectual astonishment was all the greater when one day Inma announced that we were going to learn 'seguiriyas', one of the most serious slow flamenco dances and part of the 'cante jondo' or 'deep song' style revered by aficionados. She told us it was special because its first count came on **one**, not eleven or twelve. At the start of the year I had taken it for granted that the first count was one. Now, having grown accustomed to the 'clock face' method, I found that the flavour of a flamenco style which began on the count of **one** was unusual indeed. Beginning on 1 – how daring! I felt I was seeing 'the count of one' through a new lens. Seguiriyas used the same twelve-beat structure, but was counted like this: **one** two **three** four **five** six seven **eight** nine ten **eleven** twelve. Arithmetically, this could be described as two groups of two beats, two groups of three beats, and a final pair of two. But Inma told us that wasn't the correct way to think of it: the correct way to think of, or more importantly to feel the seguiriyas was as 'a slow dance of five beats in which beats three and four are long'. I found this a delightful concept. It reminded me of a line that had greatly amused me when I was at school, when a friend wittily remarked that 'two plus two equals five, for all large values of two'. Now I felt that I was seeing 'large values of two' in practice. Feeling the sway of seguiriyas was easy if one thought of it as groups of two and large-values-of-two. It became my favourite flamenco style.

In the third term we were told that our class was to have its own cameo appearance in the end-of-year summer show, for which the school was hiring a proper theatre. We were not yet advanced enough to accompany the dancers in the authentic manner, so we were to have our own slot in which the palmas class performed its long sequence of complicated rhythms in the spirit of a 'percussion display'. The prospect of performing in public had a shrinking effect on the class, most of whom suddenly remembered that they had other commitments on the date in question. As we prepared for the show, there were fewer and fewer of us in the class, until it was basically just the dancers, the tango teacher and me. I began to regret the emphasis on the 'end product' which had frightened off our classmates. We had all enjoyed the experience of learning the 'compás' and clapping for an hour every Saturday afternoon, but performing in public was a different matter and seemed to have little to do with the learning process as such. I had the advantage of being used to performing on stage, but I was very conscious that I had no experience of the performance energy required for a flamenco show, and I think it was mostly the habit of professionalism that kept me focused. A small group of us did the show in the theatre. It was a surreal experience for me (dressed in black with a red shawl) to be on stage as part of a flamenco show, but I tried not to let myself think about how pale and comically un-Andalucían I must look under the stage lights. I kept my eyes on one of the Spanish dancers clapping beside me with a look of ferocious commitment. To my great relief, our clapping sequence was a success and quite a thrill to perform.

I had hoped to continue to 'intermediate' level , but the following year all the palmas classes were cancelled through lack of interest, and they have not been reinstated. Not wanting to cut my connection to the flamenco school, I joined the delightful Pedro's 'cajón' class to learn the technique of playing percussion on this resonant box. The action was even hotter in cajón class because by alternating the two hands on the instrument one could create much faster rhythms, rather than using both hands to produce one clap. I found however that energetically beating the hard wooden surface of the cajón was hurting my hands, so I dropped out. By that time I had joined a Spanish class and had learned enough Spanish to be able to bombard Inma with present-tense missives imploring her to start up palmas classes again.

The next year I managed to persuade Inma and her partner Danielo to come along to a concert of mine. It was the first time they had heard me 'doing my own thing'. Friends of mine were sitting near them and reported that tears were running down Inma's cheeks as she listened to me playing Schubert. Up to that point she only knew me as a beginner who couldn't or wouldn't clap loudly and who used scraps of notation to remind them of the palmas rhythms from week to week. Now she saw another side of my musical life. Hearing about her reaction was my favourite bit of audience feedback from that night, though I naturally wished that my musical accomplishment had been evident from the first in my clapping.

I continued going to the 'noches', the shows performed by the tutors and their friends. After a year's training I could grasp more of what was going on, but of course I had also become aware of how much more there was to know. My initial response to hearing the *palmeros* that first time in Seville was justified: their art of rhythm was ancient, deep and fascinating. I entertained a fantasy of becoming a proper 'palmista'. Guiding the rhythm from the still centre of the group was something that greatly appealed to me. I still felt that the *gitano* culture of flamenco was beyond my understanding, but its *music* was a language I was learning to speak. It had added new territory to my imaginative world. When I travel into town these days and pass the little side street that leads to the flamenco school, I often look down the lane and see not a faded old building but a beacon of great musicianship.

Music lights up the brain

Although my listening habits range across many kinds of music, I don't find myself dwelling on them equally. Some of them provide no more nourishment than a biscuit (and let me say straightaway that biscuitry can be found in every genre). Some kinds of music are easily digested and quickly forgotten. Others, however, appeal to the imagination in a mysterious way. The richer and more complex the music, the more I have to chew on it. Along with like-minded spirits I seem to be drawn to the kind of music which does not yield up all its secrets straightaway but which draws you into realms of discovery, working on your mind long after you've heard it. Although I like a good tune as much as anyone does, I'm drawn to what one might call ambitious music – music which aims to reflect the complexity of the lives and cultures of the people who make it. Luckily this kind of music too can be found in every category. In this book I've written about three such kinds – classical, jazz and flamenco. They are an unusual trio and I suppose it is by chance that they entered my life, but they all beckoned me into realms beyond mere entertainment or momentary distraction. They are 'high-powered' forms of music in every sense, appealing to head and heart simultaneously. They have enormous energy, but not only in a simple way.

I am fond of many kinds of music and enjoy attending performances of music from other parts of the world. Although the cultures involved may be quite different from mine, their customs and attitudes hidden from me, I never feel alienated by the *music*, which often acts as a doorway into another civilisation. Whatever type of music I'm listening to, I never tire of seeing or hearing musicality spring to life in that context. In fact, as time goes by I am more and more struck by the phenomenon of music and of how musical expression can stop us in our tracks. I know quite a lot about it and how it's done, but it remains magical.

Some say they find art forms like jazz and classical to be 'elite' and 'intimidating', but I struggle to see why. There is nothing inherently intimidating about them if they are considered purely as music. They may appeal to some kinds of minds and ears more than others, but that is perhaps more a matter of neurology or physiology than of anything else. I have intelligent, highly educated friends who seem to be insensitive to music, while on the other hand I know people who didn't thrive in formal education but are insightfully alert to music. It seems to me that there is no knowing what kind of people might be 'bitten by the music bug', and it is certainly not a matter of race, class or postcode. Chance plays a role – I often wonder what course my life would have taken if I had happened to encounter other types of music when I was growing up. One thing is certain: you cannot fall in love with music if you don't come across it in the first place, so there needs to be *opportunity*. Classical musicians are trying hard to reach out to as many audiences as they can, but it is equally important that education policy-makers provide young people with the opportunity to hear and learn to play such music.

It is a pity that sociological factors have been dragged into the argument about which kinds of music are to be encouraged and which are not. Issues of class and accessibility, for example, have played a part in classical music fading from the school curriculum and being replaced by types of music which are easy to 'have a go at' without special training. In some quarters it is considered a black mark against classical music that you need to be able to read notation to learn most of it. But learning to read music notation opens the door to many different kinds of participation in music. Who can know whether young people will need the skill at some point in their lives? Most schools do not aim to teach children to read music notation. For me this is as crazy as putting Russian on the language syllabus without teaching students to read Cyrillic script, or trying to teach algebra without using algebraic symbols. Obviously you can be a good musician without being able to read music – some of the jazz and flamenco musicians I've met are proof of that – but not being able to read music locks you out of an extraordinary repertoire. I am all in favour of improvised music, but I have never heard an improvisation which gave me the kind of long-lasting enjoyment and intellectual pleasure that my favourite works of classical music do.

Music is so lovely and such a delightful pastime that it should be the most natural thing in the world to learn it. Yet when it comes to performing complex music, there is a huge amount that has to be mastered, for performing music is an executant skill as well as one of comprehension. One might think that being a musician has a lot in common with being an actor, but whereas being an actor builds on and refines the faculties of speaking and behaving that we all naturally acquire because we are human, our lives do not prepare us in the same way for performing music. There are some types of music around the world which are easily learned and casually performed, but not the ones I've been writing about here. For those, a special synthesis of mental and physical skills is needed. Whether or not this is a good thing is something we could debate, but the fact remains that most music of enduring value is difficult to master and to perform.

It often seems extraordinary that the process of training to be a classical musician starts so early and goes on for so long. When I was at university, I remember being struck by the fact that many of my fellow students (lawyers, economists, engineers) were tackling a subject they had never studied before, and yet after only three or four years were qualified to turn professional and go straight into well-paid jobs. Compared with what happens in the world of music, three or four years seemed a shockingly brief period in which to become qualified for a lifetime's employment, and in fact I still wonder about society's evaluation of these things. Even people who have been playing their instruments since they were children often go on to do three or four years of undergraduate training followed by several more years of postgraduate education before they turn professional, or while they are turning professional. Then there are summer courses, seminars and sabbatical periods of further study. They continue to have individual lessons with teachers. They put themselves forward to play in masterclasses. As my Piano Club shows, the desire to stay close to the music one loves, to learn more music, seek more advice and keep making progress often continues through a person's adult life even if music is kept as a hobby. I would estimate that most musicians I know were 'in training' for around fifteen to twenty years. Let nobody underestimate the amount of effort involved, simply because music is an art and a vocation. Compared with this, the extended training period of medical doctors is fairly concise. It would be ludicrous to claim that being a musician is more important than being a doctor, though the two professions do have things in common. The process of learning how to be a classical musician is as long as it is because of the complexity of the music and the challenge of playing instruments to the level required for that music. When society gets around to recognising the value of music-making for mental and physical health, perhaps musicians will be as highly regarded as doctors.

I studied for longer or shorter periods with teachers in different countries: Scotland, England, France, the USA, Switzerland, Italy, Holland, Germany, Canada. They taught in a variety of settings: one-to-one lessons, performance classes involving other students, and masterclasses with an audience of the general public. As far as I know, none of my tutors had formal teaching qualifications. Some of them influenced a whole generation of successful musicians who still sigh nostalgically when they recall their lessons. Yet today those teachers would not be eligible for jobs in many schools and colleges because they did not have a teaching certificate. Even a naïve student could see that their pedagogical methods were not 'politically correct', and on occasion we all wished that there were some boundaries of etiquette they were obliged to observe. (I am not talking about the well-publicised kind of physical abuse that was discovered in some specialist music schools, which is another matter entirely, and is unacceptable.) Their 'methods' ranged from saying almost nothing to shouting, and their language skills were unreliable. Some were spellbinding 'demonstrators' while others probably played less well than their students did. Nevertheless these untrained and sometimes eccentric teachers supplied me with the most interesting, valuable and far-reaching advice of my musical life. I am not suggesting that a bit of teacher training would have ruined their brilliance, but they were teachers of another sort, more akin to the 'magi' or 'gurus' of old folk tales. I hate to think that in today's measurement-obsessed education system I would never get the chance to be taught by them. Some of the tactless and negative judgements passed in my hearing by masterclass tutors were 'wrong' and would not meet the standards of behaviour required by today's schools. But on the other hand those same teachers would not be allowed to venture into the probing psychological territory that I found so helpful when I was on the receiving end of it. I'm not sure if I would have wished to sacrifice those moments of insight for the sake of not having to suffer the insults either.

Having a step-by-step carefully calibrated method for teaching children and beginners is obviously valuable. I have never tried to teach anyone from scratch, and I have great respect for those who specialise in the skill of early-years teaching. But teaching music performance at a high level is not easily subject to a pedagogical system because being a good musician is a whole-person art. If it tends to produce unusual teachers, I can see why. Learning how to 'give' to the audience, mastering nerves, playing from memory, co-ordinating precisely with other musicians, interpreting works of music, understanding historical styles and musical idioms, learning how to control the instrument in such a way as to speak directly to the hearts of your audience in whatever size of concert hall you are playing in, learning how to trust yourself and, perhaps just as importantly, building up qualities which are worth trusting – all these challenges really amount to putting your whole self on stage. My 'gurus' were performers themselves and knew all about the kaleidoscope of thoughts and feelings that performers experience. They had, so to speak, supped from the cauldron themselves and were inclined to push others towards the heat.

My own involvement in teaching arose organically from my work as a performer. I started teaching when young musicians began to ask me how I had dealt with this or that problem in performing specific works of music. Until that point I had not thought of myself as a teacher, being content with my status as a performer and, indeed, as a learner myself. But when I started giving the occasional lesson I realised that because of my performing experience I actually knew a lot more about those works of music than the person or chamber group who had asked for my help. There *were* lots of things I could tell them or show them. Perhaps as importantly, I was active as a performer myself and so I felt that my knowledge of the music and of the issues involved in performing it was always being updated. In fact it was striking how often a recent concert of mine provided some nugget of insight or some relevant anecdote to tell my students. I felt we were all travelling the same path. My teaching activities blossomed into giving my own masterclasses and being a guest professor at various institutions and courses. My own curiosity about learning made me feel that although I had no ready-made pedagogical system, I certainly had 'knowledge content' which gave me integrity as an educator. Certain sorts of students particularly appreciated my efforts to put things into words. Some of them had been frustrated by teachers who couldn't or wouldn't do so, and preferred to gesture poetically by way of illustration. In music there are admittedly many things which are hard to speak about, but perhaps this very fact sometimes makes people lazy about trying. I was motivated to try, partly because it helped *me* to understand better.

Music is not only about emotions and feelings that can be symbolised in pantomime. It is also an expression of form. This is much harder to talk about, because music's form is articulated in the medium of time, and is not visible like a solid object. Nevertheless there is form in music, and many musicians are, like me, fascinated by it. Not every composer has been a master architect, but the great ones are. I found that when I really got under the skin of certain pieces – a late Mozart piano concerto, a Beethoven trio or a Schubert impromptu – and understood their shape and proportion, the form became a thing I could contemplate at length with the same kind of intellectual fascination that mathematicians speak of when they put their heads in their hands and visualise other dimensions. I have the impression I have thought about musical architecture more in recent years, or at least have become more able to appreciate the beauty of musical form and how it interacts with time.

I found that many students liked the fact that I was interested in listening to what they had to say as well as how they played. We had all experienced the approach of maestri who expected you to listen to what they had to say, but not to answer back. In fact, I don't think any of my (male) teachers were much good at pastoral care. I still had vivid memories of Sándor Végh, whom in other ways I greatly admired, irritably struggling to focus on a student's words on the rare occasions when someone tried to strike up a dialogue with him and make him engage with them as a person. He was so focused on imparting information to the class at large that he appeared to have forgotten the individuality of the student, whom he seemed to treat as an embodiment of some educational problem or solution. I on the other hand genuinely want to know what path has brought the student to this moment of playing to me. What do they hope to get out of it? I'm curious about their

Speaking the Piano

personal history, what made them decide to be a musician, and how they're finding life in the profession. Again, this made me different from other teachers they had encountered; when I once asked a masterclass student whether his famous professor was someone he felt he could talk to if he had a personal problem, he burst into incredulous laughter. Some of my students, on the threshold of a performing career, welcomed the chance to talk to someone who had grappled with the issues, non-musical as well as musical. I too welcomed the chance to talk, for as I mentioned elsewhere, being a pianist can be a lonely activity. I sometimes regret that it is not in my nature to provide the macho theatrical shock of some of the lessons I have witnessed, but I also recognise that people learn in different ways. Not everyone can learn in the 'school of hard knocks', and some students benefit from a more rounded approach, including an element of the pastoral care for which I myself would have been so grateful when I was a student. I hope that my advice will sink into their minds over a long period, rather than blowing the doors off. Some might say that my way of teaching is 'feminine'. If so, then perhaps such an approach is useful in a field where female teachers are under-represented at the advanced level.

I am an advocate of 'lifelong learning' and always enjoy tackling something new, but nothing has been so enriching as music. Perhaps this is because it appeals to so many different parts of one's self: physical, emotional, intellectual and spiritual. Listening to music is great, but making music yourself is even better. Some pianists might say that playing on your own is the best, but although I derive great satisfaction from playing solo recitals, I think I would say that making music with like-minded colleagues is my favourite. When you play completely on your own, information hardly reaches you from outside (some people like it that way). When you play with others, the stream of information coming to you about them and from them makes for a very rich experience. If you are interested in observing others, then there is endless food for thought in collaborating with kindred spirits, and of course making music

242

becomes a social experience too. For me, chamber music is the kind which most lights up the different parts of my musical self at the same time. Knowing how to work with other musicians to create something which is more than the sum of the parts is a special skill, a kind of 'soft power' if I could put it like that.

Being a musician has trained my mind to work differently, and perhaps with more acuity. At least I feel so, and in fact a neuroscientist once told me that there is not much that's more demanding for the brain than playing virtuoso piano music. There is something about being engaged with high-quality material at this level of detail which gradually affects the texture of your thoughts. I am not suggesting that music is the only material which can have such an effect on a person's mind – I imagine that an intense involvement with any profound art or scientific study could have a similar effect – but there is something special about music because of its extraordinary ability to link us to other dimensions. Not every little piece of music works wonders on the player, of course, but the great repertoire I have been engaged with – chamber music, solo piano music, piano concertos – has definitely acted as a mental gym. To play and perform such music takes mental, emotional, and physical powers which no performer can ever take for granted.

No big and satisfying work of music is easy to learn. It struck me recently, for example, that I had never learned Beethoven's final piano sonata, the C minor sonata opus 111. I started to learn it this month and have devoted some of each day's piano practice to it. Although I am a good sight-reader and have long acquaintance with Beethoven's piano music, learning this monumental sonata is slow going. After several weeks I have learned the notes accurately and worked out fingerings. But when I try to play everything 'up to speed', things go awry and I realise the more complicated patterns are not yet in my muscle memory. I expect this part of the process to take several more weeks with practice at gradually increasing speeds. As I go along I will be thinking about all the issues of timing, expression and touch. I hope to be able to play it 'properly' by some point in the summer, but as for memorising it, that will take longer, as there is such a mass of detail to remember, especially in the 'Arietta' variation movement. My grasp of Beethoven's musical meaning, and of how to put across the sonata's mysterious combination of resolve and serenity in performance, will probably keep unfolding for a long time to come. I have not yet scheduled the sonata for performance. This long process is not because I am a slow learner, but because the music is deep and complex. It distils the thought processes of one of the world's great creative geniuses at the height of his powers. Tackling it – or any work of similar complexity – is a training process of its own, and sometimes after a practice session I can feel the work that has been done. I cannot think of any other type of music which stretches the mind in so many directions at once.

My years of close reading have taught me how to focus on fine detail but also on large-scale thinking. You need both when you perform long and intricate works of music. Making recordings has intensified this ability to be attentive. Once you have had the experience of sitting and listening to your own recorded playing, deciding note by note what to keep, what to reject and how the 'kept' parts will relate to one another, you develop an extraordinary sort of fine-textured awareness. That extra degree of awareness has spilled over into the rest of my life. As I am not a scientist I have no basis for saying this, but I imagine that if you could map my brain activity you would find that my musical training and my instrumental expertise have increased my ability to make connections, to think fast, move fast, and to understand things on the micro- and the macro-level simultaneously. I sense that the more complex the type of music, the greater this kind of effect. Daily practice has developed my powers of concentration, and I often feel that the discipline of concentrating intensely on something is beneficial in itself. When I read in science journals that music 'lights up the whole brain' and employs large-scale neural networks, I am not in the least surprised because that is how it feels to be a musician. Playing music, thinking about it, listening to it – whether in one's head or on an external sound source – often seems to me more interesting than other things going on around me. I don't mean that I use music as a retreat, although it may look that way to some. I mean that it offers a sort of heightened awareness which enables one to hear the music in many things. Quite honestly, I cannot understand why music is not amongst the subjects which our society and government most cherish and make provision for young people to learn.

At the time of writing, music has been downgraded from being a core subject in the UK school curriculum. Learning an instrument has become unavailable in some schools, an 'add-on' in others. Many children can only learn an instrument if their parents are in a position to organise and pay for private lessons, and they have the challenge of acquiring an instrument too. Yet at the same time there is a constant stream of research praising the effects of music education on children's minds. All the evidence points towards the fact that learning music enhances cognitive skills. It teaches pattern recognition, counting skills, critical thinking, self-discipline, and even some of the tools used in conflict resolution. It enables self-expression through the medium of art, and it provides us with emotional expression which can be cathartic. It develops the ability to use both hands with equal fluency, it sharpens reflexes, and it gives us insight into the wonderful way that a craft can become an art. A skill which benefits young people in every way, from physical co-ordination through aesthetic understanding to awareness of others, could hardly be more important. I suspect its downgrading is partly because musical attainment is difficult to measure and difficult for a computer to assign marks to, but to set it aside as a consequence is the ultimate in short-term thinking. While many of the 'facts' we spend so much time learning at school will be forgotten or prove unnecessary for our adult lives, a multi-faceted skill such as music goes on giving – and not only to the individual.

As Michele Hanson wrote in *The Guardian* in December 2015, 'If you want to encourage co-operation, collaboration, socialising, civility, creativity, responsibility and self-confidence, don't bother with citizenship classes. Just have an orchestra. Or any musical group. They'll do all of that and more. And playing in one makes you feel good. I know because I do it. It's a lifesaver.' For many people the importance of music is, of course, far beyond the sum total of the 'skill-sets' it offers. I recently received a letter from someone who asked if I would be willing to give her some piano lessons even though her playing was restricted by having had operations on both hands. Surprisingly, she was working towards playing a piano recital in public. She wrote, 'I wonder if I'm daft to think about playing. It's just that when I do play, I feel more alive than at any other time.' Many would agree with her.

In this book I've written about different teaching methods I've encountered, ranging from the orthodox to the eccentric. All of them were useful to me in one way or another. There are many ways of learning and teaching music, and there will always be many ways, because music is too big a thing to pin down and codify. Its nature is to escape our grasp. We create music, but we are also mystified by what we have created, and we want to follow where music leads. Perhaps the most useful thing that teachers can do, therefore, is to kindle a fire which will light the young musician's path as they set out on their own journey of discovery, a journey which leads inwards as well as outwards.

Epilogue

Like Janus, this book looks in two directions: from the perspective of a teacher and from the perspective of a learner. I sometimes feel as if alongside my performing career I have spent most of my life being either a student or a teacher, often both at the same time. One of the things I like about the music world is that the people I work with are rarely set in their ways and almost never regard themselves as being 'the finished article' with nothing more to learn.

'Lifelong learning' has rightly become a buzzword in adult education, but the concept is nothing new to musicians, who can easily find themselves still on the receiving end of advice while at the same time advising younger musicians. I have given public masterclasses while simultaneously taking lessons myself as a beginner in another type of music such as jazz. I have played in a masterclass one day and taught the same repertoire to younger musicians the next. Chamber music is a big part of my life and in chamber music you have to be able to notice what other people are doing, and what they are trying to do. This kind of music is collegial, driven by sharing and debate. In rehearsals there is very little recognition of 'seniority'; everyone feels free to comment on everyone else's playing, so I am always taking in new information from fellow instrumentalists of all ages. There is a sort of continuum of shared experience which passes back and forth and makes music a fertile ground for lifelong discovery.

I think that people outside the music world sometimes look at musicians with wonderment when they see how we strive to remain open to criticism and ready to try new approaches. To those outsiders, musicians probably seem unstable creatures who can't settle to anything and seem to have an inadvisable lack of self-respect. This is partly due to the well-documented fragility of music as a career. Musicians – especially those in classical solo and chamber music – are keenly aware of the fact that they are only as good as their most recent concert, and that day after day their skills need to be demonstrable. It is no good having been superb when you were a college laureate or a competition winner. You have to be able to play well 'tomorrow, and tomorrow, and tomorrow'. I think this goes some way to accounting for the apparently fickle way that musicians build up obsessively to a concert, put it behind them as soon as it's over and start building up obsessively to the next. They know that it is all very well being able to say that you played well in your last concert, but will you play well in the next one? Your skills have to be kept active. This can make musicians seem as if they are living in an eternal present, which probably makes some people view them as childlike. On the plus side, musicians often have a flexibility of mind which keeps them young. I smile to remember sitting with Sándor Végh (then in his seventies) on a hotel terrace in Switzerland, watching senior citizens perambulating up and down in the sunshine. Végh made a face and said, 'Ugh. I don't like being surrounded by these *old people*.' He was the same age as many of them, but he certainly didn't seem to be of their company. He seemed far more 'juvenated', if that is a word. When you met his eye you knew he had not lost interest in life.

As a teacher myself, I have never been able to cast aside the learner's perspective and feel like an oracle untroubled by memories of what it is like to be taught. Many renowned teachers seem to have forgotten what they were like as nervous youngsters. When I was a student, my friends and I had a phrase for such tutors: 'one-way channel'. They spoke and we listened. We sensed that they had walked away from us to a lofty mountaintop from which they passed down edicts. Perhaps being aloof was a necessary act of self-preservation to shut themselves off from their students' neediness, or perhaps they really felt that they had vanquished whatever insecurities they had had as younger musicians and had earned the right to be Olympian.

Although I do have moments when I feel that way myself, I am usually conscious of the fact that we musicians are all travelling the same path, with some of us further along it than others. It even feels as if one can turn and walk back to an earlier point on the path in order to keep someone company. Because of my performing experience and the amount of time I have spent pondering the issues that music raises, I do know more than my students, but I don't feel fundamentally *different* from them. I am still pondering many of the things they ponder. I see myself as giving them information about the part of the road they haven't travelled yet, being in dialogue with them and hopefully hearing interesting things from them about their journey as well. I know that having a more 'seigneurial' style of teaching would save time and energy, but it doesn't seem to suit my nature. Whenever I have tried it, I have felt lonely. So perhaps it is for my sake as well that I pursue a more open-minded approach to teaching.

It's often assumed that a teacher is a great teacher if their students are successful. Of course the success of students *may* indicate excellent teaching, but it may simply indicate that famous names tend to attract excellent students. I have known many people who studied with 'big name' teachers but felt discouraged by the lack of individual attention. You can learn things even if you are not the focus of attention, but it should not only be up to the student to make a success of the experience. There are probably too many elite institutions using star professors to attract talented students whose achievements reflect credit on the institution, even if the star professor is absent on long tours, bored by the minutiae of teaching, or too busy with their own career to help their students devise career strategies of their own (and of course this problem is not unique to music).

I'm sometimes asked in which 'school of piano' I was trained, but I don't know how to answer that question as none of my piano teachers ever mentioned a tradition to which they felt they belonged. If I am part of a tradition, it is the one that Sándor Végh often spoke about when he told his students it was important they become conscious of their place in a chain of European musicians stretching across the generations, carrying an imaginative and 'speaking' approach to music. But I do not have a particular sound I want my piano students to make. Instead, I want them to cultivate an enquiring mind. Rather than focusing directly on them or their piano technique, I focus on what is in the score, what I think the composer hoped for, and how the player can achieve it. In exploring those things, we address a whole range of technical issues, but we address them in context rather than in isolation. I find that in trying to think about what the composer meant, we are not restricting our range of expression but, on the contrary, often expanding it because we are putting our imaginations to work empathetically.

When someone's playing is unconvincing, it is usually because they haven't noticed what is in the score. A page of music is flat. Were it to be a relief map or a three-dimensional model, the composer might have a better chance of indicating the ups and downs of the music, the different layers and slopes, the roads and the meadows, the things which are in plain sight as opposed to in shadow. Often the ingredients missing from someone's performance are actually indicated in the score if they would only take the trouble to look and to ask themselves how those things might give light and shade to the performance. Of course there are things beyond the notes, but they are accessed through the notes, not invented out of nothing. With good music, one can be sure that there is a powerful creative imagination at work and a persuasive way of bringing the music to life if one harnesses one's own imagination to the task. I want students to train themselves to be sensitive to the qualities and character of the music, and to clear away anything which gets in the way. This means encouraging them to be thoughtful about all the aspects of music – melody, harmony, rhythm, timing, dynamics – which are under a performer's influence. In a sense it means encouraging them to be ego-less. Students sometimes say, 'Shouldn't I try to put my personality into the performance?' My answer is that there is no way of keeping it out. Personality is not something you need to strive to make the audience notice, for your physical presence and body language will make them aware of it anyway.

I have spent years grappling with these issues and questions for one simple reason: that music (classical music in particular) is of fundamental importance to me. Of course there is nothing 'simple' about it. Why is music so important to me, and to people who share my love for it? It is often said that music 'is a metaphor for life' and it is true that in music we recognise powerful analogies for emotional processes we experience in our own lives. We hear a lot these days about the mind-expanding qualities and immersive powers of 'virtual reality', and perhaps music is a special kind of virtual reality. However, I feel that music is more than that. To say that music is a metaphor would suggest that music is not part of life but merely a representation of it for illustrative purposes. This is not how music feels when you are playing it or being carried away by it as a listener. It does not only give you intellectual satisfaction. Especially when played live, in the same physical space as you, the soundwaves of music actually impact on you. Music can affect your breathing rate, your pulse, your adrenalin and the alpha waves in your brain. When someone makes music, it *is* a thing which is happening now, and the feelings expressed can be felt now. It *is* part of life. I am not suggesting that if music makes you feel happy, it means that you are happy in general, or that if music makes you feel sad it is the same kind of sadness as when a bad thing happens in everyday life, but nevertheless I would contend that the shock of happiness, sadness or energy that music can make you feel is real. I agree it is mysterious, but it is what makes music so powerful for so many. I see the effect of live music at the end of each meeting of my Piano Club when people are reluctant to leave because they have one more thing they want to say about why they love Schumann, or whoever. When people sit there listening to one another and dabbing away tears, it is not because they admire the music intellectually. It's because they are actually touched. For me this makes music more than metaphor. All the people who listen over and over again to their favourite songs are not doing so merely because the music *reminds them* of a feeling of yearning they had at some other time; they are in touch with that feeling as they listen because music embodies the yearning.

Index